PRIVACY IN EMPLOYMENT: CONTROL OF PERSONAL INFORMATION IN THE WORKPLACE

KRIS KLEIN

VIVIAN GATES

© 2005 Thomson Canada Limited

NOTICE AND DISCLAIMER: All rights reserved. No part of this publication may be reproduced, stored in a retrieval system, or transmitted, in any form or by any means, electronic, mechanical, photocopying, recording, or otherwise, without the prior written permission of the publisher (Carswell).

Carswell and all persons involved in the preparation and sale of this publication disclaim any warranty as to accuracy or currency of the publication. This publication is provided on the understanding and basis that none of Carswell, the author's or other persons involved in the creation of this publication shall be responsible for the accuracy or currency of the contents, or for the results of any action taken on the basis of the information contained in this publication, or for any errors or omissions contained herein. No one involved in this publication is attempting herein to render legal, accounting, or other professional advice.

Library and Archives Canada Cataloguing in Publication

Klein, Kris
   Privacy in employment : control of personal information in the workplace / Kris Klein and Vivian Gates.

Includes bibliographical references.
ISBN 0-459-24281-4

   1. Privacy, Right of–Canada.   2. Personnel records–Law and legislation–Canada.   I. Gates, Vivian.   II. Title.

KE1240.K54 2005   342.7108'58   C2005-905284-8
KF1262.K54 2005

One Corporate Plaza, 2075 Kennedy Road, Toronto, Ontario M1T 3V4
Customer Relations:
Toronto 1-416-609-3800
Elsewhere in Canada/U.S. 1-800-387-5164   www.carswell.com
Fax 1-416-298-5082   carswell.orders@thomson.com

Foreword

No relationship in the world of privacy is so fraught with difficulties as the one between employer and employee. From the issues of control over personal information to the question of employee surveillance, the tensions are constant and seemingly unrelenting.

Part of the problem lies in the obvious power imbalance in the relationship, and part in the economic imperatives of the bottom line in the marketplace.

This book is timely because the issues it considers are at the forefront of the privacy debate, here in Canada, the U.S. and Europe. Advances in technology, which touch all of us have the potential to affect employees as a group of citizens even more. Increasingly it is easy for employers to use these technologies for example, to improve productivity, to cut down on employee theft, and even in some circumstances actually to "manage" employees. Employees for their part find themselves fighting for dignity in the workplace.

Neither side in this *struggle* is always necessarily right or wrong, and both must work to find a balance that recognizes the competitive advantages technology can provide, and yet preserve the fundamental right of individuals to be treated with respect.

"Privacy in Employment – control of personal information in the workplace", thoroughly explores the employer/employee relationship and privacy issues, and it will serve as a valuable resource for all who must deal with that complex, delicate and evolving relationship.

August 31, 2005

Heather Black

Preface

Whereas the notion of privacy has been around for centuries, it has gained a certain degree of significance since the advent of the "information age". The struggle to control personal information is emerging as individuals, corporations, associations, unions and lawmakers place a newfound value on information that reveals details about people. Nowhere is this struggle more evident than in the workplace. The obvious tension between employer and employee is the perfect arena for two players to spar over who should have control over personal information. As in many relationships, employers and employees need and depend on each other. Nonetheless, there exists within this symbiotic agreement a constant struggle to "get more" from the relationship. Each party partakes. Management wants to improve efficiency, promote the right people, cut costs, prevent theft and harassment, etc. Employees want to remain autonomous human beings, be treated with dignity, be promoted fairly, and reveal only that information about themselves that will aid their cause. It is inevitable for the two sides to eventually clash over privacy rights.

The law of privacy in Canada is admittedly in its infancy. Jurisprudence is far from complete and it is not even entirely clear where and how the law protects privacy. A myriad of provincial, federal and common laws do provide a patchwork of helpful guidelines, but uncertainty remains. Determining when exactly one interest will prevail over the other remains a difficult task. Continuing technological advances, varying degrees of employee organization, changing economic pressures and continued expectations to create profit and efficiency come together every day in new ways creating new contexts and new tensions. From the traditional "hiring of a private detective to determine if an employee's allegations of injury are valid", to the futuristic "genetic testing of employees to determine long term suitability for employment", to the perpetually controversial practice of monitoring employees' use of email or internet - what is certain is that the tug-o-war over workplace privacy continues to broaden and take on new significance.

The employment context does provide, because of the particular differences in interests amongst the parties, a clear window into how the law is answering questions about which contexts will allow certain interests to prevail. This book looks through that window and explores the debate raging in the workplace. We have endeavoured to provide a no-nonsense look at what questions have been asked and how they were answered, and combine it all into a useful tool for those who need to know the jurisprudence to date.

By studying how the law has currently tackled the issues, some predictions might be made for the situation the reader might find themselves in presently or in the future. While uncertainty remains, we hope this study of what has been decided up until now will prove a useful mechanism to guide employers and employees alike through the emerging privacy-related problems they may face in the workplace.

Kris Klein
Vivian Gates

July 2005

Table of Contents

Foreword iii
Preface v
Table of Cases xi

1 DATA PROTECTION AND PRIVACY LEGISLATION – GENERALLY
1.1 Overview 1
1.2 Federal Legislation 2
    1.2.1 Public Sector 2
    1.2.2 Private Sector 3
    1.2.3 Office of the Privacy Commissioner of Canada 5
1.3 Provincial Legislation 6
    1.3.1 Public Sector 6
    1.3.2 Private Sector 6
    1.3.3 Regulatory Bodies 7

2 HIRING PROCEDURES
2.1 Interviewing 9
2.2 Résumés/Portfolios/Documentation 10
2.3 Staff Input/Consultation 11
2.4 Background Checks 12
2.5 Psychological & Aptitude Testing 16

3 EMPLOYMENT RECORDS
3.1 Introduction 19
3.2 Work Performance 19
3.3 Personnel Files 21
3.4 Disciplinary Records 23
3.5 Criminal Records 25

4 WORK PRODUCT & PROFESSIONAL INFORMATION
4.1 Work Product 27
4.2 Professional Information 30

5 PERSONAL OPINIONS IN EMPLOYMENT
5.1 Introduction 33
5.2 Personal Opinions in the Public Sector 35
    5.2.1 Opinions and Views viz the Employer 35
    5.2.2 Opinions and Views viz Colleagues 39
    5.2.3 Third Party Access to Opinions of Employer/Employees 41
5.3 Personal Opinions in the Private Sector 44

6   PERSONAL SEARCHES OF EMPLOYEES 47

7   MONITORING AND SURVEILLANCE
7.1   E-Mail Monitoring 51
    7.1.1   Introduction 51
    7.1.2   Reasons for Monitoring E-Mail 51
    7.1.3   Legality of Monitoring 52
        (a)   American Approach 53
            (i)   Electronic Communications Privacy Act 53
            (ii)   Common Law Tort of Invasion of Privacy 55
        (b)   Canadian Approach 56
            (i)   Criminal Code 57
            (ii)   Canadian Jurisprudence 58
    7.1.4   E-Mail as Discovery Material 63
    7.1.5   Effect on Employees 64
    7.1.6   Establishing an E-mail Policy 65
7.2   Video Surveillance 66
    7.2.1   Introduction 66
    7.2.2   Reasons Cited for Using Video Surveillance 66
    7.2.3   Video Surveillance in the Workplace 67
    7.2.4   Video Surveillance outside the Workplace 73
    7.2.5   Emerging Surveillance Issues 80

8   MEDICAL AND GENETIC INFORMATION
8.1   Medical Information 85
    8.1.1   Introduction 85
    8.1.2   Mandatory Medical Examinations 85
    8.1.3   Medical Certificates 88
    8.1.4   Medical Records 91
    8.1.5   Monitoring & Surveillance / Surveillance as Evidence 94
8.2   Genetic Information & Privacy 94
    8.2.1   Introduction 94
    8.2.2   Legislation 96
    8.2.3   Screening, Monitoring and Discrimination: Implications on Hiring, Job Retention and Promotion 97
    8.2.4   Impact on Eligibility for Health Benefits, Long Term Disability and Life Insurance 101
    8.2.5   The Tension between the Potential Benefits and Harms of Genetic Testing 103

DRUG TESTING & PRIVACY
9.1   Drug Testing 105
    9.1.1   Introduction 105

TABLE OF CONTENTS

	9.1.2	Is Drug Testing an Invasion of Privacy?	106
	9.1.3	The American Approach	106
	9.1.4	The Canadian Approach	108
		(a) The Charter of Rights and Freedoms	108
		(b) Canadian Human Rights Act	109
		(c) Arbitration	117

10 DISCLOSURE OF EMPLOYEE INFORMATION
10.1 Disclosure to Unions 123
10.2 Disclosure to Boards/Tribunals/Courts 125
10.3 Disclosure to other Third Parties 128

10 CONCLUSION 135

Table of Cases

A.T.U., Local 569 v. Edmonton (City), 2004 ABQB 280, 2004 CarswellAlta 435 (Alta. Q.B.) 77
Air Canada v. C.A.L.E.A., (1981), 4 L.A.C. (3d) 68 (Can. Arb. Bd.) 24
Air Canada v. C.U.P.E., [1995] C.L.A.D. No. 114 (Can. Arb. Bd.) 74
Alberta Wheat Pool v. Grain Workers' Union, Local 333 (1995), 48 L.A.C. (4th) 332 (B.C. Arb. Bd.) at 341 73
Amalgamated Electric Corp. (Markham) v. I.B.E.W., Local 1590 (1974), 6 L.A.C. (2d) 28 (Ont. Arb. Bd.) 47, 48
B.C. Teacher's Federation v. B.C. Public School Employers' Association, [2002] L.C.C. No. 4454 90
Battlefords & District Co-operative Ltd. v. Gibbs, [1996] 3 S.C.R. 566 (S.C.C.) 102
Becker Milk Co. and Milk & Bread Drivers, Dairy Employees, Caterers & Allied Employees, Local 647, Re (1996), 53 L.A.C. (4th) 420 (Ont. Arb. Bd.) 94
Bell Canada c. S.C.E.P., (2000), 2000 CarswellNat 3866 (Can. Arb. Bd.) 59
Bell Canada v. C.T.E.A. (2000), 2000 CarswellNat 1389, [2000] R.J.D.T. 358 (Fed. T.D.), affirmed 2001 FCA 139 (Fed. C.A.) 59
Bhamre Employment Insurance Claim Appeal, (September 23, 1998), CUB 42012A 60
Billings v. Atkinson, 489 S.W.2d 858 (Tex., 1973) 55
Blood Tribe (Department of Health) v. Canada (Privacy Commissioner), 2005 FC 328 5
Board of School Trustees of School District No. 44 (North Vancouver) 44
Board of School Trustees of School District No. 84 (Vancouver Island West) .. 41
Bourke v. Nissan Motor Corp. No. YC003979 (Cal. Sup. Ct., Los Angeles County, 1991) 56
Briar v. Canada (Treasury Board), 2003 PSSRB 3 (Can. P.S.S.R.B.) 61
Briggs v. American Air Filter Co., 630 F.2d 414 (5th Cir., 1980) 54
British Columbia (Public Service Employee Relations Commission) v. B.C.G.S.E.U. (1999), 176 D.L.R (4th) 1 (S.C.C.) 111, 112, 113
Calgary (City) v. A.T.U., Local 583 (1997), 61 L.A.C. (4th) 317 (Alta. Arb. Bd.) 23
Canada (Information Commissioner) v. Canada (Commissioner of the Royal Canadian Mounted Police) [2003] 1 S.C.R. 66 (S.C.C.) 23, 29
Canada (Information Commissioner) v. Canada (Commissioner of the Royal Canadian Mounted Police) (sub nom. Canada (Information Commissioner) v. Canada (Commissioner of the Royal Canadian Mounted Police)) [2003] 1 S.C.R. 66 (S.C.C.) [Canada v. Commissioner of the RCMP] 130
Canada (Information Commissioner) v. Canada (Immigration & Refugee Board) (1997), 1997 CarswellNat 2436, [1997] F.C.J. No. 1812 (Fed. T.D.) 41
Canada (Information Commissioner) v. Canada (Minister of Citizenship & Immigration) [2003] 1 F.C. 219 (Fed. C.A.) 39

Canada (Information Commissioner) v. Canada (Solicitor General) [1988] 3 F.C. 551 (Fed. T.D.) 42
Canada (Privacy Commissioner) v. Canada (Attorney General), 2003 BCSC 862 (B.C. S.C.) 5
Canada Post Corp. v. C.U.P.W., (1990), 10 L.A.C. (4th) 393 (Can Arb. Bd.) ... 48
Canadian Civil Liberties Assn. v. Toronto Dominion Bank (1994), 22 C.H.R.R. D/301 (Can. Human Rights Trib.), reversed (1996), (sub nom. Canadian Human Rights Commission v. Toronto Dominion Bank) 112 F.T.R. 127, 25 C.H.R.R. D/373 (Fed. T.D.), reversed (1998), 163 D.L.R. (4th) 193, 32 C.H.R.R. D/261 (Fed. C.A.) 109, 110
Canadian Pacific Ltd. v. B.M.W.E. (1996), 59 L.A.C. (4th) 111 (Can. Arb. Bd.) 76, 80
Canadian Pacific Ltd. v. U.T.U., (1987), 31 L.A.C. (3d) 179 (Can. Arb. Bd.) 118, 119
Central Alberta Dairy Pool v. Alberta (Human Rights Commission), [1990] 2 S.C.R. 489 (S.C.C.) 111
Chambly (Commission scolaire régionale) c. Bergevin, (sub nom. Commission scolaire régionale de Chambly v. Bergevin), [1994] 2 S.C.R. 525(S.C.C.) 111
Consumers Gas v. C.E.P. (1999), [1999] O.L.A.A. No. 649 (Ont. Arb. Bd.) at para. 71 61
Crump v. Beckley Newspapers Inc., 320 S.E.2d 70 (W.VA., 1983) 55
Dagg v. Canada (Minister of Finance), [1997] 2 S.C.R. 403 (S.C.C.) .. 27, 30, 131
Dickie v. Nova Scotia (Department of Health) (1999), 1999 CarswellNS 97, [1999] N.S.J. No. 116 (N.S. C.A.) 43, 131
Doman Forest Products Ltd. v. I.W.A., Local 1-357 (1990), 13 L.A.C. (4th) 275 (B.C. Arb. Bd.) 60, 74, 75
Drug Trading Co. & Druggists Corp. v. E.C.W.U., Local 11 (1988), 32 L.A.C. (3d) 443 (Ont. Arb. Bd.) 49
Duncanson v. Toronto (Metropolitan) Police Services Board, (1999), [1999] O.J. No. 2464, 1999 CarswellOnt 2013 (Ont. Div. Ct.) 129
Eastmond v. Canadian Pacific Railway. 2004 FC 852, 2004 CarswellNat 1842 (F.C.) 70, 71
Entrop v. Imperial Oil Ltd. (1996), 24 C.C.E.L. (2d) 122 (Ont. Bd. of Inquiry), affirmed (1998), 35 C.C.E.L. (2d) 56 (Ont. Div. Ct.), leave to appeal allowed (1998), 1998 CarswellOnt 1955 (Ont. C.A.), reversed (2000), 189 D.L.R. (4th) 14 (Ont. C.A.) 111, 112, 115
Esso Petroleum Canada v. C.E.P., Local 614, (1994), 56 L.A.C. (4th) 440 (B.C. Arb. Bd.) 119
Flanagan v. Epson America Inc. (1990) SWC 112749 56
Fraser v. Nationwide Mutual Ins. Co., Case No. 98-CV-6726 (E.D. Pa., 2001) 54
French v. Dalhousie University (2003), 2003 CarswellNS 40, [2003] N.S.J. No. 44 (N.S. C.A.) 40

TABLE OF CASES

Garrity v. John Hancock Mutual Life Insurance Co. (U.S. Dist. Ct. (Mass.), May 7, 2002) 56
Glenbow-Alberta Institute v. C.U.P.E., Local 1645 (1988), 3 L.A.C. (4th) 127 (Alta. Arb. Bd.) 48
Greater Vancouver Regional District v. G.V.R.D.E.U. (1996), 57 L.A.C. (4th) 113 (B.C. Arb. Bd.) 75
H.R.E.U., Local 448 v. Millcroft Inn Ltd. (2000), [2000] O.L.R.D. No. 2581, 2000 CarswellOnt 3073 (Ont. L.R.B.) 7 online QL (LRBD) 123
I.U.O.E, Local 793 v. Sarnia Cranes Ltd., [1999] O.L.R.B. Rep. 479 (Ont. L.R.B.) 120
IMS Health Canada 34
Jackson v. Joyceville Penitentiary, [1990] 3 F.C. 55 (Fed. T.D.) 108
K-Mart Canada Ltd. v. S.E.I.U., Local 183 (1981), (sub nom. S.E.I.U., Local 183 v. K-Mart Canada Ltd.) 81 C.L.L.C. 16,084 (Ont. L.R.B.) 68
Labatt Ontario Breweries (Toronto Brewery) v. Brewery, General & Professional Workers Union, Local 304 (1994), 42 L.A.C. (4th) 151 (Ont. Arb. Bd.) 68, 74, 75
Lavigne v. Canada (Commissioner of Official Languages), [2002] 2 S.C.R. 773 (S.C.C.) 35
L'Ecuyer c. Aéroports de Montréal, 2003 FCT 573, 2003 CarswellNat 1286, 2003 CarswellNat 2621 (Fed. T.D.), affirmed 2004 CarswellNat 4173, 2004 CAF 237 (F.C.A.) 70
Lenworth Metal Products Ltd. v. U.S.W.A., Local 3950 (2000), 2000 CarswellOnt 4282 (Ont. Div. Ct.) 68
Lornex Mining Corp. v. U.S.W.A., Local 7619 (1983), 14 L.A.C. (3d) 169 (B.C. Arb. Bd.) 49
Lovelock v. DuPont Canada Inc. (1998), 1998 CarswellOnt 4626, [1998] O.J. No. 4971 (Ont. Gen. Div.) 64
Lumber & Sawmill Workers' Union, Local 2537 v. KVP Co. (1965), 16 L.A.C. 73 (Ont. Arb. Bd.) 49, 60, 118
MacNeil v. R., [2002] FCT 277, [2002] F.C.J. No. 363 (Fed. C.A.) 22, 25, 30
Masterfeeds and U.F.C.W., Local 1518, (2000), 92 L.A.C. (4th) 341 (B.C. Arb. Bd.) 89
McInerney v. MacDonald [1992] S.C.R. 138 (S.C.C.) 91
Merck & Co. v. Apotex Inc., [1996] 2 F.C. 223 (Fed. T.D.), affirmed (1996), 1996 CarswellNat 100, 1996 CarswellNat 1763 (Fed. C.A.), leave to appeal refused (1997), 1997 CarswellOnt 6337 (S.C.C.) 63
Monarch Fine Foods Co. v. Milk & Bread Drivers, Dairy Employees, Caterers & Allied Employees, Local 647 (1978), 20 L.A.C. (2d) 419 (Ont. Arb. Bd.) ... 47
Nader v. General Motors Corp., 255 N.E.2d 765 (N.Y., 1970) 55
National Automobile, Aerospace, Transportation and General Workers Union of Canada v. Canadian National Railway Company, Labour Arbitration News, September/ October, 2000 (M. Picher) 120
NAV Canada v. C.A.T.C.A., Re (1998), 74 L.A.C. (4th) 163 (Can. Arb. Bd.) .. 87

Nesbitt Burns Inc. v. Lange (2000), 2000 CarswellOnt 1296, [2000] O.J. No. 335 (Ont. S.C.J.) 64
New Flyer Industries Ltd. v. CAW-Canada, Local 3003 (2000), (sub nom. New Flyer Industries Ltd. v. C.A.W.-Canada, Local 3003) 85 L.A.C. (4th) 304 (Man. Arb. Bd.) 74
Newfoundland Light & Power Co. v. I.B.E.W., Local 1620 (1990), 13 L.A.C. (4th) 341 (Nfld. Arb. Bd.) 24
Northwest Territories v. Union of Northern Workers (2001), [2001] N.W.T.J. No. 24, 2001 CarswellNWT 29 (N.W.T. S.C.) 124
NRS Block Brothers Realty Ltd. v. Co-operators Development Corp., (1994), 24 C.P.C. (3d) 132 (Sask Q.B.) 63
O.P.S.E.U. v. Ontario (Management Board Secretariat), (2003), 117 L.A.C. (4th) 128 15
O.S.S.T.F., District 25 v. Ottawa-Carleton District School Board. (2001), [2001] O.L.R.D. No. 4575, 2001 CarswellOnt 4902 (Ont. L.R.B.) 123
O'Malley v. Simpsons-Sears Ltd., (sub nom. Ontario Human Rights Commission v. Simpsons-Sears Ltd.), [1985] 2 S.C.R. 536 (S.C.C.) 111
Ontario Human Rights Commission v. Dofasco Inc. (2001), [2001] L.C.C. No. 406, 208 D.L.R. (4th) 276 (Ont. C.A.) 91
Ontario Human Rights Commission v. Etobicoke (Borough) [1982] 1 S.C.R. 202 (S.C.C.) 86
Ontario Nurses' Association v. North York General Hospital, (2004), [2004] O.L.A.A. No. 109, 2004 CarswellOnt 1723 (Ont. Arb. Bd.) 92
Ontario Nurses' Association v. St. Joseph's Hospital [2002] O.L.A.A. No. 869 89
P.S.A.C. v. Canada (Treasury Board) (April 26, 1996), Doc. 161-2-791, 169-2-584, [1996] C.P.S.S.R.B. No. 30 (Can. P.S.S.R.B.) 124
Pacific Northwest Herb Corp. v. Thompson, (1999), 1999 CarswellBC 2738, [1999] B.C.J. No. 2772 (B.C. S.C.) 58
Procor Sulphur Services v. C.E.P., Local 57 (1998), 79 L.A.C. (4th) 341 (Alta. Arb. Bd.) 120
Progistix-Solutions Inc. v. C.E.P., Local 26 (2000), 89 L.A.C. (4th) 1 (Ont. Arb. Bd.) 49, 50
Provincial-American Truck Transporters v. Teamsters Union, Local 880 (1991), 18 L.A.C. (4th) 412 (Ont. Arb. Bd.) 118
Puretex Knitting Co. v. C.T.C.U., (1979), 23 L.A.C. (2d) 14 (Ont. Arb. Bd.) ... 68
Quebec (Commission des droits de la personne et des droits de la jeunesse) v. Boisbriand (City) [2000] 1 S.C.R. 665 (S.C.C.) 97
R. v. Chatham (1985), 23 C.R.R. 344 (B.C. S.C.) 108
R. v. Cremascoli (1979), (sub nom. R. v. Goldman) [1980] 1 S.C.R. 976 (S.C.C.) 60
R. v. Dyment [1988] 2 S.C.R. 417 (S.C.C.) 99, 108
R. v. Sanelli, (sub nom. R. v. Duarte) [1990] 1 S.C.R. 30 (S.C.C.) 60
R. v. Weir, (1998), 59 Alta. L.R. (3d) 319 (Alta. Q.B.), affirmed (2001), 156 C.C.C. (3d) 188 (Alta. C.A.) 63

TABLE OF CASES

Reichmann v. Toronto Life Publishing Co., (1988), 66 O.R. (2d) 65 (Ont. H.C.) 63

Renaud v. Central Okanagan School District No. 23, (sub nom. Central Okanagan School District No. 23 v. Renaud), [1992] 2 S.C.R. 970 (S.C.C.) 111

Richardson v. Davis Wire Industries Ltd. (1997), 28 C.C.E.L. (2d) 101 (B.C. S.C.) 67

Robertson v. Canada (Minister of Employment & Immigration) (1987), 13 F.T.R. 120 (Fed. T.D.) 33

Ross v. Rosedale Transport Ltd., (2003), 2003 CarswellNat 3620, [2003] C.L.A.D. No. 237 (Can. Arb. Bd.) 78

School District No. 39 (Vancouver) v. B.C.T.F. (2003), 224 D.L.R. (4th) 63 (B.C. C.A.), leave to appeal refused (2003), 109 C.R.R. (2d) 188 (note) (S.C.C.) 87

Shell Canada Products Ltd. v. Canadian Association of Industrial, Mechanical & Allied Workers, Local 112, Re (1990), 14 L.A.C. (4th) 75 (B.C. Arb. Bd.) 87

Simons v. Prince Edward Island (Workers' Compensation Board) (2000), 2000 CarswellPEI 47 (P.E.I. C.A.) 125

SKF Manufacturing of Canada Ltd. v. I.A.M., Local 901 (1975), 9 L.A.C. (2d) 139 (Ont. Arb. Bd.) 24

Skinner v. Railway Labour Executives' Assn., 489 U.S. 602 (U.S. Cal., 1989) 107

Smyth v. Pillsbury Co., 914 F. Supp. 97 (U.S. Dist. Ct. E.D. Penn., 1996) 55, 56

Societé canadienne des postes c. S.P.C. (January 31, 1995), Bergeron Arb. (Can. Arb. Bd.) 124

Society of Professional Engineers & Associates v. Atomic Energy of Canada Ltd., [2001] C.I.R.B.D. No. 7, [2001] C.I.R.B. No. 110, 2001 CarswellNat 3651 (C.I.R.B.) 124

Steels Industrial Products v. Teamsters Union, Local 213 (1991), 24 L.A.C. (4th) 259 (B.C. Arb. Bd.) 75

Steve Jackson Games Inc. v. United States Secret Service, 36 F.3d 457 (5th Cir., 1994) 54

Tandy Electronics Ltd. v. U.S.W.A., [1979] O.L.R.B. Rep. 248 (Ont. L.R.B.), affirmed (1979), 79 C.L.L.C. 14,216 (Ont. Div. Ct.)) 68

Tiberino v. Spokane County No. 18830-2-III (Wash. App. Div. 3) 64

Tillbury Assembly Ltd and United Auto Workers, Local 251, (2004), 124 L.A.C. (4th) 375 (Ont. Arb. Bd.) 90

Toronto District School Board and C.U.P.E., Local 4400, (2002), 109 L.A.C. (4th) 20 (Ont. Arb. Bd.) 127

Toronto Transit Commission v. A.T.U., Local 113 (1999), 95 L.A.C. (4th) 402 (Ont. Arb. Bd.) 74

Transit Windsor v. A.T.U., Local 616 (2001), 99 L.A.C. (4th) 295 (Ont. Arb. Bd.) 79

Trimac Transportation Services - Bulk Systems v. T.C.U. (1999), 88 L.A.C. (4th) 237 (Can. Arb. Bd.) 115
U.A.W., Local 444 v. Chrysler Corp. of Canada, (1961), 11 L.A.C. 152 (Ont. Arb. Bd.) [hereinafter Chrysler] 47
U.A.W., Local 707 v. Ford Motor Co. of Canada (1971), 23 L.A.C. 96 (Ont. Arb. Bd.) 69
U.F.C.W., Local 401 v. Economic Development Edmonton (2002), [2002] A.L.R.B.R. No. 41, 2002 CarswellAlta 1031 (Alta. L.R.B.), application for stay denied (2002), [2002] A.J. No. 800, 2002 CarswellAlta 799 (Alta. Q.B.) 124
Union of Canadian Correctional Officers c. Conseil du Trésor, 2002 PSSRB 58 (Can. P.S.S.R.B.) 124
United States v. Simons, 29 F.Supp.2d 324 (E.D. Va., 1998) 56
United States v. White, (1970), 401 U.S. 745, at 787-89 65
University Hospital v. London & District Service Workers' Union, Local 220 (1981), 28 L.A.C. (2d) 294 (Ont. Arb. Bd.) 49
Walbar Canada Inc. v. U.S.A., Local 9236, Dated April 22, 1993, unreported .. 75
Watkins v. L.M. Berry & Co., 704 F.2d 577 (11th Cir., 1993) at 582-585 54
Wesely College v. Pitts 1974 F. Supp. 375 (D. Del., 1997) 54
West Park Hospital and ONA (1993), 37 L.A.C. (4th) 160 (Ont. Arb. Bd.) 93
Western Grocers v. U.F.C.W.U., Local 1400 (unreported) a Saskatchewan decision dated July 21, 1995 77

1

Data Protection and Privacy Legislation – Generally

1.1 OVERVIEW

Canada's legal framework for privacy issues in relation to employment and the workplace comprises a wide scope of legislation and jurisprudence. This spectrum includes constitutional law (i.e. the *Canadian Charter of Rights and Freedoms*[1]), quasi-constitutional law (i.e. Quebec's *Charter of Human Rights and Freedoms*[2]), federal and provincial/territorial human rights codes, federal and provincial/territorial data protection and privacy statutes, provincial health information protection legislation, laws governing professional confidentiality, workers' compensation law, employment standards legislation, the criminal law (i.e. protections against physical intrusion), statutory privacy torts in certain provinces, and the emerging common law tort of invasion of privacy. Against this backdrop, it should be noted that the *Canadian Charter of Rights and Freedoms* applies only to governments and private sector bodies acting as agents of government, and any provision within federal, provincial or territorial legislation that is inconsistent with the Charter is of no force or effect.

While all of these laws combined play a vital role in balancing the competing interests of employees and employers with respect to privacy issues at work, depending on the nature of each circumstance, it is beyond the scope of this book to conduct an in depth study of each legislative area. The foregoing statutes and common law are briefly addressed in relation to specific topics throughout this book; therefore, the discussion will be limited to a general overview of federal and provincial/territorial data protection and privacy legislation in Canada as it applies to employees and employers in the workplace.

---

[1] *Charter of Rights and Freedoms*, Part I of the *Constitution Act, 1982*, being Schedule B to the *Canada Act 1982* (U.K.), 1982, c. 11.

[2] *Charter of Human Rights and Freedoms*, R.S.Q. c. C-12.

1.2 FEDERAL LEGISLATION

1.2.1 Public Sector

The federal *Privacy Act*[3] of 1982 regulates the collection, use and disclosure of personal information by federal government institutions, including government employers, and controls the rights of individuals to access personal information held by those agencies. "Personal information" under this Act is broadly defined as "information about an identifiable individual that is recorded in any form", subject to certain exclusions. Most of the *Privacy Act*'s protection does not apply to personal information that is publicly available, to personal information placed in the National Archives of Canada or other federal public libraries by persons or organizations other than government institutions.

Government institutions may only collect personal information which relates directly to an operating program or activity and is intended to be used for an administrative purpose. Wherever possible, personal information should be collected directly from the individual to whom it relates, and the individual should be informed of the purpose for which their personal information is being collected, unless there is a concern that informing the individual might result in the collection of inaccurate personal information, or defeat the purpose or prejudice the use for which the information is collected. Personal information must be retained by an institution for such period of time after its use to ensure that the individual to whom it relates has a reasonable opportunity to obtain access to that information. The institution must take reasonable steps to ensure that the personal information used for an administrative purpose is as accurate, complete and up-to-date as possible.

Personal information under the control of the government may be used by the institution without the consent of the individual to whom it relates if it is used for the purpose for which the information was compiled, or for a use consistent with a that purpose. The government institution may not disclose the personal information without the consent of the person to whom it relates unless the disclosure falls within the specified exceptions under section 8(2) of the Act. The head of a government institution must retain a record of any use or disclosure by the institution of personal information contained in a personal information bank, except where such use is in connection with an investigative body specified in the regulations for the purpose of enforcing any law of Canada or carrying a lawful investigation, where the investigative body provides a written request identifying the

---

[3] *Privacy Act*, R.S.C. 1985, c. P-21.

purpose and describing the information to be disclosed. Each government institution must also publish at least once a year a comprehensive index of personal information banks maintained by the institution, and make the publication available throughout Canada via Canadian Government Publishing (commonly referred to as InfoSource) and the Internet.

The *Privacy Act* also grants Canadian citizens and all individuals present in Canada a mandatory right of access to their personal information upon request to a government institution. To access non-personal information controlled by a government institution, individuals may apply via the provisions of the federal *Access to Information Act*[4] provided that the institution is subject to this Act. Following an individual's request for access to personal information under the *Privacy Act*, a government institution has 30 days after receiving the request to respond to the applicant, with the option to extend the response time to an additional 30 days if reasonably necessary. Where an individual is refused access, the head of the government institution must justify the basis upon which access had been denied. The head of the institution may also refuse to indicate whether or not the personal information actually exists, in which case, the applicant must be informed of the provisions of the *Privacy Act* that would allow for an exemption if the personal information did in fact exist.

Pursuant to the exemption provisions of the *Privacy Act*, an applicant may be denied access to personal information where the head of the institution has a reasonable expectation that the use of this information would cause probable harm or another consequence specified in the exempting provision. In addition, certain personal information banks may be designated as exempt banks to which a head of government may also refuse right of access where disclosure may be injurious to international affairs and defence, national security, the conduct of police investigations and other lawful inquiries, and the enforcement of any law in Canada.

1.2.2 Private Sector

The federal *Personal Information Protection and Electronic Documents Act*[5] ("*PIPEDA*") came into effect on January 1, 2001 and regulates how private sector organizations (including associations, partnerships, persons, and trade unions) may collect, use or disclose personal information in the course of commercial activities that fall within federal jurisdiction. The Act also applies to personal information about employees of organizations that the organization collects, uses or discloses in connection with the

---

[4] *Access to Information Act,* R.S.C. 1985, c. A-1.
[5] *Personal Information Protection and Electronic Documents Act,* S.C. 2000, c. 5.

operation of a federal work, undertaking or business. *PIPEDA* permits the collection, use or disclosure of personal information by these organizations "for purposes that a reasonable person would consider appropriate in the circumstances". Exceptions to its scope include personal information collected, used or disclosed for personal, domestic, journalistic, artistic, literary or non-commercial purposes.

Part 1 of the Act establishes parameters for the collection, use, disclosure, retention, and disposal of personal information.[6] *PIPEDA* broadly defines "personal information" as information, recorded or otherwise, about an identifiable individual, with the exception of the name, title, business address, or business telephone number of an employee of an organization. To constitute personal information, the data must be linked to a specific, natural person. While personal information need not be recorded to be protected under the Act, records include any correspondence, memorandum, book, plan, map, drawing, diagram, pictorial or graphic work, photograph, film, microform sound recording, videotape, machine-readable record, and any other documentary material, regardless of physical form or characteristics, and any copy of any of those items.

Part 1, which is where privacy protection is found, reflects 10 core principles from the Canadian Standards Association's "Model Code for the Protection of Personal Information" that organizations must comply with when processing personal information, namely, identification of purposes, accountability, openness, consent, limiting collection, limiting use, disclosure and retention, individual access, security safeguards, accuracy, and compliance.

PIPEDA requires organizations to identify the purposes for which personal information is collected, at or before the time the information is collected, and ensure that the knowledge and consent of the individual has been obtained for the collection, use or disclosure of personal information, except where inappropriate as specified under the legislation. Further, an organization must limit the collection, use and disclosure of personal information to that which is necessary for the purposes identified, unless it obtains the express consent of the individual, or is required to provide the information by law. Organizations are obliged to retain personal information only for as long as is necessary to fulfill those purposes, and personal information must be kept as accurate, complete, and up-to-date as is necessary for the purposes for which it is to be used. Personal information must

---

[6] Parts 2 through 5 deal with the use of electronic transactions and documents to facilitate business with the federal government electronically, assist electronic communication and submission of records in judicial proceedings, and disseminate federal government publications by electronic means.

also be protected by security safeguards appropriate to the sensitivity of that information.

An organization is required to adhere to principles of openness and accessibility by making available to individuals specific information about its policies and practices relating to the management of personal information. The organization must inform an individual of the existence, use and disclosure of his or her personal information upon written request, and must give the individual access to that information. An individual may challenge the accuracy and completeness of the information and have it amended as appropriate. The organization must provide a mechanism by which an individual may address a challenge concerning compliance with the aforementioned principles. Finally, the CSA Model Code emphasizes accountability of organizations responsible for personal information under their control, thus, an organization should designate a Chief Privacy Officer, or the equivalent, to be accountable for the organization's compliance with its privacy policies and the fundamental principles of *PIPEDA*.

1.2.3 Office of the Privacy Commissioner of Canada

The Office of the Privacy Commissioner is an independent body which oversees both the *Privacy Act* and *PIPEDA* and reports to Parliament on an annual basis. The Commissioner has broad powers to investigate, compel evidence, issue subpoenas, access internal documents (including those otherwise protected by solicitor-client privilege[7]), mediate, and make recommendations regarding a complaint of invasion of privacy. However, he/she does not have the authority to issue orders or penalties to remedy the alleged violation, or to initiate a Charter challenge in relation to a breach of privacy.[8] Investigations must be conducted by the Commissioner in confidence, and evidence provided thereof is not admissible against the parties in Court or in any other proceeding. However, the Commissioner may, on reasonable notice and at any time, conduct audits of an organization's personal information management practice if he/she has reasonable grounds to believe that the organization has contravened a provision in Part 1, and may reveal to the public details of an organization's practices where he/she determines that it is in the public interest to do so.

The complainant is entitled to a report of the Commissioner's findings following the completion of an investigation, and if a complainant is dis-

---

[7] See, however, *Blood Tribe (Department of Health) v. Canada (Privacy Commissioner)*, 2005 FC 328 (F.C.).
[8] *Canada (Privacy Commissioner) v. Canada (Attorney General)*, 2003 BCSC 862 (B.C. S.C.).

satisfied with the Commissioner's decision, he or she has the right to seek judicial review of the matter by the Federal Court of Canada. Where the Court deems it appropriate, it may, in addition to providing other remedies, order an organization to correct its practices in order to comply with the legislation; order an organization to publish a notice of any action taken or proposed to be taken to correct its practices; and award damages to the complainant, including damages for humiliation. The Commissioner can also initiate a review by the Federal Court of Canada in limited circumstances involving denial of access to records.

1.3 PROVINCIAL LEGISLATION

1.3.1 Public Sector

All provincial and territorial legislatures have enacted general data protection and privacy legislation to regulate the collection, use and disclosure of personal information by public sector bodies, although these laws and the levels of privacy protection vary significantly from one jurisdiction to another. Unlike the federal regime, the provinces and territories address access to information rights and privacy rights under the same statute in the respective jurisdictions, New Brunswick being the exception. Quebec in particular has enacted a broad range of privacy laws which cover both the public and private sectors. Most notably in the public sector, section 5 of the province's *Charter of Human Rights and Freedoms* enshrines the right to privacy as a fundamental individual right by prescribing that "Every person has a right to respect for his private life".

1.3.2 Private Sector

As of January 1, 2004, *PIPEDA* was extended to every organization which collects, uses and discloses personal information in the course of any commercial activity, including provincially regulated organizations, unless the province which regulates the organization enacts laws "substantially similar" to *PIPEDA*. To date, only Quebec, British Columbia and Alberta have been determined to be substantially similar in privacy legislation in the private sector, therefore, all other provincial organizations that collect, use and disclose personal information in the course of any commercial activity fall within the purview of *PIPEDA*. Personal information controlled by agents of the provincial Crown and by private sector organizations conducting activities *other than* commercial enterprise in provinces without substantially similar legislation is not protected under *PIPEDA*, thereby leaving certain individuals susceptible to violations of privacy.

1.3.3 Regulatory Bodies

Oversight bodies range widely in scope and powers between the provinces, from simply providing an Ombudsman for the entire region to the establishment of a dedicated office with a Privacy Commissioner and trained staff. Unlike the *Privacy Act*, some provincial data protection legislation, such as that of British Columbia, Alberta, Ontario, and Quebec, prescribes powers for adjudicators to make enforceable orders. However, the decisions of adjudicators are subject to judicial review by the provincial trial and appeal courts.

2

Hiring Procedures

2.1 INTERVIEWING

Human rights legislation provides the legal framework that proscribes practices by employers in all matters relating to prospective employment which may deprive individuals of employment opportunities on the prohibited grounds of discrimination enumerated in respective federal and provincial human rights statutes. Such practices may include inappropriate questioning on an application for employment or during a job interview which directly or indirectly classifies or indicates qualifications by a prohibited ground of discrimination. The same line of questioning, though not designed to discriminate or exclude, could arguably extend to invasion of a candidate's privacy as well, and may not necessarily be relevant to the position sought by the applicant.

Federal and provincial privacy legislation makes clear that employers may collect personal information only for purposes that relate directly to an operating program or activity of the institution, or that a reasonable person would consider appropriate in the circumstances. The federal *Privacy Act* regulates the collection, use and disclosure of personal information of any individual by the federal government institutions, which are defined as all of the government departments, bodies and offices listed under the schedule of Government Institutions.

The *Privacy Act* protects an employee's personal information from unauthorized collection, use and disclosure. For a government employer to collect personal information, that personal information must relate directly to an operating program or activity of the institution and where possible, the employer must collect the personal information from the employee directly. In accordance with section 8(1) of the *Privacy Act*, when information is collected without the employee's consent, disclosure of that personal information is restricted to the purposes for which it was collected, or to use consistent with that purpose, unless it falls under the exceptions in section 8(2) of the *Privacy Act*.

Currently, *PIPEDA* applies to every employer that collects, uses and discloses personal information in the course of a commercial activity unless those employers are located in a province that has enacted legislation deemed substantially similar to *PIPEDA*.[1] *PIPEDA*, however, would still be applicable to employers in those provinces when personal information crosses provincial borders or, arguably, when it passes to federal bodies and to federal works.

Personal information means any information about an identifiable individual, but does not include the name, title or business address or telephone number of an employee of an organization. Unlike the *Privacy Act*, *PIPEDA* does not include an enumerated list to illustrate the specific meaning of personal information, therefore, one could infer that all information "about an identifiable individual" would be considered personal information for the purposes of *PIPEDA*. In other words, personal information should be given a broad and liberal meaning.

The purpose of *PIPEDA* is similar to that of the *Privacy Act*, except that the activity in question is between an employee and an employer in the private sector. The purpose is defined under section 3 which can be distilled to mean that rules that govern the collection, use or disclosure of personal information balances the interests of the employee's right to privacy with those of the employer's need to collect, use or disclose personal information for purposes that a reasonable person would consider appropriate.

Additionally, the Canadian Human Rights Commission has established comprehensive guidelines for employers regarding the type of information obtainable from applicants during the interview process without inviting a human rights complaint or possibly one of invasion of privacy.[2] These guidelines specifically caution employers from eliciting extraneous information from applicants to assess their candidacy for a position.

2.2 RÉSUMÉS/PORTFOLIOS/DOCUMENTATION

Employers regularly collect from prospective employees various types of documentation, such as résumés, portfolios, and university transcripts, which are considered personal information protected by privacy statutes if these relate to an identifiable individual. Employers also often receive unsolicited documentation from eager applicants, implying collection with

---

[1] Currently, only Alberta (*Personal Information Protection Act*, S.A. 2003, c. P-6.5), British Columbia (*Personal Information Protection Act*, S.B.C. 2003, c. 63), and Quebec (*An Act Respecting The Protection Of Personal Information In The Private Sector*, R.S.Q. c. P-39.1) have enacted legislation that has been deemed substantially similar to *PIPEDA*.

[2] Canadian Human Rights Commission, "Guide to Screening and Selection in Employment", April 1999, online: <http://www.chrc-ccdp.ca/publications/screening_employment-en.asp>.

consent since the information is voluntarily submitted to the employer. Arguably, candidates who are asked to provide specific documentation prior to or in conjunction with being interviewed consent to divulging their personal information in part as a condition of employment.

Privacy legislation prescribes that such information may only be used for the purpose for which it was collected, that is, one which relates directly to an operating program or activity of the institution or that a reasonable person would consider appropriate in the circumstances, such as considering an individual for a position within the organization. The employer is also obligated to secure the information in an appropriate manner, which might entail placing the documentation in a personnel file for new hires, or perhaps destroying it within a reasonable time frame if the candidate is not selected for employment.

2.3 STAFF INPUT/CONSULTATION

Privacy legislation clearly outlines an employer's obligations to collect, use, disclose, and secure the personal information of employees and potential employees only for purposes that a reasonable person would consider appropriate in the circumstances, or for a purpose that relates directly to an operating program or activity of the institution. This raises questions of propriety regarding access by non-management colleagues to an applicant's personal information (for example, résumés, portfolios, and other documentation) in the hiring process. Moreover, should non-supervisory colleagues participate in or conduct job interviews, and be consulted in the hiring of candidates? Generally, non-management colleagues play a lesser role or no role after hiring with regard to coworkers' performance reviews, pay raises, promotions, discipline, and termination, which supports the view that the employer-employee relationship is highly personal and usually exclusive of others not privy to a respective employment contract. Interestingly, these principles appear to be more flexible in the hiring process, despite the fact that candidates may consider their preliminary documentation to be no less personal and no less worthy of privacy protection from coworkers who may be their professional equals in the workplace.

The following case illustrates one example of an employee's personal information being exposed to co-workers by the employer, albeit legitimately, but without the employee's consent. The team manager at a telecommunications company shared a telemarketer's sales figures with coworkers without her consent, prompting her to file a complaint with the Privacy Commissioner. The employee considered her work performance and sales commission to be confidential and had not received any explanation regarding the purpose of collecting and displaying employees' sales statistics. The company alleged that all new employees were informed of this practice and that the purpose of this practice, which was to motivate employees and encourage competition in order to increase sales, had been reiterated at numerous staff meetings. The company maintained that this was a proven and accepted practice in sales and that the posting of employee sales results was also a widely accepted practice among telemarketers. Further, the company did not consider sales figures to be personal information since they were produced in the course of business activities, and even if it was found to be personal information, reasonable use of such information in the workplace should not require the express consent of employees.

The Commissioner found that sales statistics are personal information pursuant to *PIPEDA,* as they constitute information about an identifiable individual. However, although the complainant did not expressly consent to the practice of displaying sales statistics, the complainant had implied her consent by willingly participating in a business environment where the practice of disclosing employees' personal sales results could reasonably be expected. The Commissioner did recommend that the company take steps to ensure that all telemarketing employees were clearly informed of the company's practices and its purposes for disclosing personal sales records.[3]

2.4 BACKGROUND CHECKS

Employers generally use background checks to verify the accuracy of information provided to them by job seekers, and to uncover information not acquired in the application or interview. However, such investigations are subject to various federal and provincial statutes designed to protect an individual's privacy rights.

Credit checks may be conducted both on potential and current employees where the employee is or will be performing their duties in a position of trust or financial responsibility. In these circumstances, employers must notify the individual in writing that they are conducting a credit check and identify the consumer reporting agency that will be providing the credit check, pursuant to section 10(2) of the *Consumer Reporting Act*, R.S.O. 1990, c. C.33. Some consumer reporting agencies have access to information regarding, for example, a person's character, reputation, health, physical or personal characteristics and lifestyle. Thus, employers must be mind-

---

[3] Privacy Commissioner of Canada, September 15, 2003, Summary #220.

ful to not use such information in a way that may discriminate against or invade an individual's privacy.[4]

A complaint brought before the Privacy Commissioner of Canada by a bank customer illustrates the point that employers do not have unlimited entitlement to an employee's credit information. The employer in this case had not acted inappropriately, rather, a collections officer contracted by a bank allegedly disclosed a customer's credit card and outstanding debt to her employer, though the officer swore an affidavit that she had never spoken to the employer. Instead, the officer accused the employer of covering for the complainant with regard to the outstanding debt. When the Commissioner's office investigated the matter, the employer corroborated the employee's accusations against the officer and the Commissioner determined that the bank had not conducted a proper investigation, having failed to consult with the complainant's employer. The bank indicated numerous ways in which the agency had not met its contractual obligations to the bank with respect to the bank's privacy and confidentiality policy, which was to inform an employer of an employee's financial problems, in accordance with the section 7(3)(b) debt collection provision of PIPEDA, only when legal action was required to garnish an employee's wages. The bank subsequently implemented punitive measures and subjected the agency to a detailed audit.[5]

Employers may ask for references and undertake employment history checks, however, those who do ask for references can incur liability for failing to check those references in the event of an employee's improper acts.[6] Security checks, which often also encompass criminal record checks, may be done where an employer can establish that they are reasonable and relevant to the position, and where the prospective employee consents to the check. Employers can ask on an application form whether the applicant has been convicted of a criminal offence for which a pardon has *not* been granted, however, prior to the interview stage employers may not ask about the applicant's record of offences regarding provincial statutes. While an employer can refuse to hire an applicant based on their criminal record if no pardon has been granted, human rights legislation prohibits against

---

[4] Ogilvy Renault, "Employee Background Checks", October 2002 [*Ogilvy Renault*]; McCarthy Tétrault LLP, "Privacy in the Workplace" by D. Lynne Watt, January 2002, online: <http://www.mccarthy.ca./pubs/publication.asp?pub_code=650>.
[5] Privacy Commissioner of Canada, April 24, 2003, Summary #168.
[6] *Ogilvy Renault, supra,* note 4.

discrimination in employment on the grounds of conviction for a provincial offence or for an offence for which pardon has been granted.[7]

The Privacy Commissioner has heard numerous complaints against employers regarding security checks. In one case, 35 employees of a company's nuclear products division filed a complaint after the Canadian Nuclear Safety Commission ordered its licensed companies to ensure that all persons who entered a licensed facility first had security clearance. The employees each received an information package that included consent forms describing the type of information being collected, the purpose for the collection, and details of a confidentiality agreement between the collection firm and the company. However, the employees complained that their consent to the security check was not meaningfully voluntary since employees who consented and failed the security check would likely be reassigned, and those who refused consent could lose their job.

The Commissioner determined that the company had ensured that it would not collect personal information without the employees' express consent, and despite the possibility of negative consequences with or without consent, the security check was still voluntary as the employees always had a choice. The security check was deemed appropriate by a reasonable person in the circumstances due to the Canadian Nuclear Safety Commission notification that it would revoke its companies' licences if they did not comply, and due to increased concern over terrorist attacks against nuclear facilities.[8]

Another complaint involved allegations by an employee that his employer had forced him to consent to a security check enabling him to work in a restricted area at an airport. The security check was required in accordance with federal government policy, which necessitates all persons working in restricted areas in all of its airports to submit to a security check. The employee had signed a form when first hired acknowledging the possibility of a security clearance and the possible repercussions should an employee refuse. However, the employee claimed that his subsequent consent was neither informed nor voluntary since he had signed the consent form after being suspended for three days and being threatened with dismissal. The Commissioner found that the company had initially informed the employee at the time of hiring that a security check may be required and that failure to consent could result in dismissal; that the employee did have a choice in the matter despite the potentially negative consequences; that it was reasonable for the airport to require security clearance given the increased

---

[7] *Supra*, note 2.
[8] Privacy Commissioner of Canada, August 14, 2002, Summary #65.

threat of terrorism; and that a reasonable person would deem it appropriate for a company to comply with federal requirements.[9]

In *O.P.S.E.U. v. Ontario (Management Board Secretariat)*,[10] the union applied for interim relief in connection with two other grievances relating to the employer's plans to implement employee security checks. The purpose of the security checks was to establish the same level of security certification of employees as that existing federally in connection with information that was exchanged between the two levels of government. The union sought an order prohibiting the employer from proceeding with the process until the Grievance Settlement Board had disposed of the grievances. The grievances dealt with the unilateral implementation of security checks by the employer without consultation with the bargaining agent, despite documentation indicating that consultation meetings were planned to discuss bargaining agent feedback to the proposed policy and implementation.

The draft policy stated that an employee who refused to consent to a security check would be removed from the position requiring security clearance, and if security clearance was not granted, the employee would not be able to remain in that position. In balancing the convenience to the employer against the potential harm to employees, the arbitrator ruled that there was no indication that the province's ongoing relationship with its federal counterparts was in jeopardy if things remained *status quo* pending the resolution of the grievances. Conversely, the questioned integrity of employees who might be displaced because of an unsatisfactory security check could not be undone. Thus, the union was granted interim relief as the privacy interests of the employees outweighed those of the employer in the particular circumstances of this case.

At issue in a case involving a commercial airline pilot was a request by the pilot's employer that pilots sign an authorization form, required by the United States government, to disclose personnel information of Canadian pilots to the U.S. government indicating that the pilots had received requisite training on aircraft simulators twice a year to maintain their professional certification. The Privacy Commissioner held that the form did not meet fair information principles and the airline's reasons for requiring its pilots to sign the form were unreasonable. It was inappropriate to require pilots to consent to collection and disclosure practices that contravened Canadian law, and since Canadian pilots had already received security clearance, a reasonable person would be unlikely to find it appropriate to

---

[9] Privacy Commissioner of Canada, March 4, 2003, Summary #127.
[10] (2003), 117 L.A.C. (4th) 128 (Ont. C.E.G.S.B.).

force pilots to disclose their personal information at the request of a foreign government.[11]

2.5 PSYCHOLOGICAL & APTITUDE TESTING

In Canada, the use of psychological tests is not prohibited and is popular amongst employers to screen prospective employees or assess the suitability of an employee to a particular job. These tests include a wide range of instruments, such as general intelligence tests, aptitude tests, performance tests, personality tests, honesty tests, handwriting analysis. Pre-employment testing is permitted if the purpose of the test is to measure the individual's inherent ability to perform certain job requirements. However, the validity of such tests has been questioned due to possible built-in cultural and gender biases.[12] Human rights legislation prohibits testing that is linked to an individual's characteristics rather than to specific ability to perform job functions. For example, the *Canadian Human Rights Act*[13] states:

> 8. It is a discriminatory practice
>
> . . .
>
> > (b) in connection with employment or prospective employment, to publish any advertisement or *to make any written or oral inquiry*
>
> that expresses or implies any limitation, specification or preference based on a prohibited ground of discrimination.
>
> 9. (1) It is discriminatory practice for an employee organization on a prohibited ground of discrimination
>
> . . .
>
> > (c) to *limit, segregate, classify* or otherwise act in relation to an individual in a way that would deprive the individual of employment opportunities, or limit employment opportunities or otherwise adversely affect the status of the individual, where the individual is a member of the organization or where any of the obligations of the organization pursuant to a collective agreement relate to the individual.

---

[11] Privacy Commissioner of Canada, December 19, 2002, Summary #106.
[12] Information and Privacy Commissioner of Ontario, "Workplace Privacy: The Need for a Safety-Net", November 1993, online: <http://www.ipc.on.ca/scripts/index_.asp?action=31&P_ID=11439&N_ID=1&PT_ID=11351&U_ID=0#testing>.
[13] *Canadian Human Rights Act*, R.S.C. 1985, c. H-6.

Aptitude tests, for example, must be appropriately connected to the position in question that the individual has applied for and must not violate human rights law. However, because aptitude tests are not reliable indicator of the quality of future job performance, it is very difficult for an employer to demonstrate a valid and useful relationship between the test results and the performance of a particular job function. Further, aptitude tests are often discriminatory, therefore, by implementing these tests, employers risk making hiring decisions based on unreliable information and may be exposing themselves to claims of human rights violations.[14]

Likewise, the use of psychological testing requires employers to show that the test results are linked to specific job requirements and must not include extraneous, irrelevant, or discriminatory information relating to the individual's psychological make-up. Studies indicate that the most important and useful role for pre-employment psychological testing is that it can expose a candidate's character as honest or dishonest.[15]

---

[14] McCarthy Tétrault LLP, "Privacy in the Workplace", *supra*, note 4.
[15] *Ibid.*

3

Employment Records

3.1 INTRODUCTION

Federal and provincial labour/employment standards legislation requires employers to keep and maintain employee records for varying periods, depending on the jurisdiction, statute, and the type of information placed in the record. Privacy legislation generally prohibits collection, use and disclosure of personal information, including the personal information contained in employee records, without the knowledge and consent of the individual, unless it relates directly to an institution's operating program or activity or to a purpose which a reasonable person would consider appropriate in the circumstances.

3.2 WORK PERFORMANCE

Decisions by the Privacy Commissioner of Canada suggest that personal information of employees and company information are not always mutually exclusive. However, these decisions emphasize that while *PIPEDA* recognizes the needs of organizations to use personal information in the workplace, the Act does not allow for uses that are unreasonable, unnecessary or poorly defined.

A telemarketer at a telecommunications company filed a complaint with the Commissioner that her team manager had shared her personal information, specifically, her sales figures, with co-workers without her consent. She considered her work performance and sales commission to be confidential and had not received any explanation regarding the purpose of collecting and displaying employees' sales statistics. The company alleged that all new employees were informed of this practice and that the purpose of this practice, which was to motivate employees and encourage competition in order to increase sales, had been reiterated at numerous staff meetings. The company maintained that this was a proven and accepted practice in sales and that the posting of employee sales results was also a widely accepted practice among telemarketers. Further, the company did not consider sales figures to be personal information since they were produced in the course of business activities, and even if it was found to be personal information, reasonable use of such information in the workplace should not require the express consent of employees.

The Commissioner found that sales statistics are personal information pursuant to *PIPEDA*, as they constitute information about an identifiable individual. However, although the complainant did not expressly consent to the practice of displaying sales statistics, the complainant had implied her consent by willingly participating in a business environment where the practice of disclosing employees' personal sales results could reasonably be expected. The Commissioner did recommend that the company take steps to ensure that all telemarketing employees were clearly informed of the company's practices and its purposes for disclosing personal sales records.[1]

In another case involving a telecommunications company, two former employees complained that their employer had collected statistics about their work without their consent and had subsequently used this personal information to assess their work performance. The company asserted that it was company practice to collect information regarding the volume, duration, and type of call received by its operators to manage individual work performance, and that this practice was communicated to employees in a variety of ways, including disclosure of individual statistics each month. The Commissioner determined that a reasonable person would conclude that it is proper for a company to monitor and assess its employees' work performance and that it is proper to use statistical information in connection with the calls to measure their performance. The employer had informed the employees and by virtue of working for a company, the employees had given implicit consent to work performance evaluations.[2]

By contrast, the Privacy Commissioner of Canada's earlier decision in *IMS Health Canada* (see Chapter 5 – **Personal Opinions**), suggests a lack of consistency in assessing what specifically constitutes personal information in relation to the professional information of employees obtained by employers as compared to the foregoing cases. In response to a complaint filed by a physician against IMS Health Canada alleging that the company was selling information about the prescribing patterns of physicians without their consent, the Privacy Commissioner held that the prescribing patterns of physicians did not comprise personal information about the physician. Rather, the Commissioner stated that a prescription in relation to an identified patient is personal health information about that patient, and not the physician. Further, a prescription is the outcome of professional interaction between the physician and patient and thus is more appropriately regarded

---

[1] Privacy Commissioner of Canada, September 15, 2003, Summary #220.
[2] Privacy Commissioner of Canada, April 14, 2003, Summary #153.

as work product. With regard to the bodies covered by *PIPEDA*, the Commissioner stated that "to interpret personal information so broadly as to include work products could allow for the inclusion of documents written by employees in the course of employment, reports prepared by employees for managers' use, or legal opinions, and would therefore be inconsistent with the stated purpose of *PIPEDA*".

3.3 PERSONNEL FILES

Privacy legislation and decisions by the Privacy Commissioner indicate that requests by individuals to access their personal information should not be unreasonably withheld, and that reasons for denying access should be limited and specific.

Two employees who unsuccessfully competed for another position at an airport requested a copy of their personnel files to determine why they did not win the competition. The employer initially denied their request to see the files but eventually allowed them access five months after the request, which was well beyond the 30-day time limit prescribed in *PIPEDA*. When the individuals complained to the Privacy Commissioner, the Commissioner determined that the employer had contravened the Act. The employer agreed to place scores obtained in a job competition in the employee file, and retain the file for a period of six months following the competition.[3]

In another private sector case, an individual suing his former employer for wrongful dismissal and breach of contract complained that the employer did not respond to his request within the 30-day time-limit. Further, though the company released some of the documents, it failed to provide him with all of his personal information. The employer claimed that the cost of responding to the request was too costly and likened the former employee's request to a "forensic audit". The company opposed granting access because the employee was suing the employer and believed that his request was directly linked to the lawsuit. The company did provide the employee with some of his personal information several months after the access request, however, the Assistant Privacy Commissioner found that the employer failed to provide the employee with information about him contained in minutes from meetings of the board of directors around the date of his dismissal. The company argued that the employee was seeking the documents in question to circumvent the disclosure and production rules under the *Rules of Civil Procedure*, and that the minutes from board meetings were confidential and should not be made available.

---

[3] Privacy Commissioner of Canada, October 22, 2002, Summary #87.

3.3 PRIVACY IN EMPLOYMENT

The Assistant Privacy Commissioner determined that since nearly six months had passed since the initial access request, the employer was deemed to have refused access contrary to *PIPEDA*. The Assistant Privacy Commissioner also found that the company had contravened the Act by imposing a $1,500 access fee, which was not a minimal amount pursuant to requirements under the Act, and that some of the complainant's personal information had in fact not been provided to him. Moreover, in differentiating the scope of discovery from the scope of an access to personal information request, the Assistant Privacy Commissioner informed the employer that with respect to their claim regarding the employee's attempts to circumvent the legal process, whereas discovery requires each party to disclose all facts and information before trial, PIPEDA grants a right of access to all personal information which an employer retains about an individual whether the information is relevant or not.[4]

In *MacNeil v. R.*,[5] the Federal Court ruled that providing poor references does not constitute a breach of an employee's privacy. In this case, an RCMP officer who had resigned from the force filed an action against the RCMP for damages for malicious conspiracy and breach of privacy following his unsuccessful application to six other police forces and for re-engagement with the RCMP, and the placement of assault charges against him in his personnel file. The officer claimed that he had been promised a positive reference by his RCMP supervisor upon his resignation, however, the supervisor denied he had made such an offer because of the officer's poor performance. Although the officer had authorized the other police forces to contact the RCMP for employment references, his RCMP supervisor provided him with poor references when contacted by the forces because the officer had not fulfilled his commitment to serve anywhere in Canada and had never completed his field training.

The Court held that there was no defamation or malicious conspiracy by the RCMP to ruin his career. The officer had failed to appreciate that other police forces did not find him to be an attractive candidate given his poor performance and his criticism of the RCMP during his interviews. Moreover, all negative notes had been removed from the officer's personnel file before his application for re-engagement with the RCMP was considered. The supervisor had not breached the officer's privacy rights since the officer had authorized the other police forces to contact the RCMP for references.

The Supreme Court of Canada has emphasized that while information about government employees may be considered personal information as

---

[4] Privacy Commissioner of Canada, December 21, 2004, Summary #285.
[5] [2002] FCT 277, [2002] F.C.J. No. 363 (Fed. C.A.).

defined by the *Privacy Act*, such information must be disclosed if it directly relates to the general characteristics associated with the position or function of a federal employee and to understanding the functions performed by those employees.

The issues in *Canada (Information Commissioner) v. Canada (Commissioner of the Royal Canadian Mounted Police)*[6] pertained to freedom of information and the right to inspect public documents containing personal information. In connection with litigation against four RCMP officers, an individual had requested information from the RCMP about the officers, including a list of the officers' historical postings, their status and date, the list of ranks and when they achieved those ranks, their years of service, their anniversary dates of service, and any public complaints made against the officers. The RCMP refused the request on the basis that the records constituted "personal information" as defined under section 3 of the *Privacy Act*, and therefore were exempt from disclosure pursuant to section 19(1) of the *Access to Information Act*, R.S.C. 1985, c.A-1.

The Federal Court of Appeal held that only information regarding a public servant's current or most recent position had to be released, however, on appeal to the Supreme Court of Canada, the Supreme Court ruled that although the information did qualify as "personal information" pursuant to the Act, the RCMP must disclose all of the information requested by the individual. The exception under section 3(j) of the *Privacy Act* applied, allowing disclosure because the information was directly related to the general characteristics associated with the position or function of a federal employee. The information did not reveal anything about the competence of the officers or divulge any personal opinion given outside the course of employment, rather it provided information relevant to understanding the functions performed by the officers. The Court also held that the information applied retroactively and was not limited to an employee's most recent position.

3.4 DISCIPLINARY RECORDS

Arbitration decisions indicate that all prior incidents of discipline can form part of an employment record, unless the collective agreement contains a sunset clause requiring the expunging of such incidents after a specified period of time. Prior acts of misconduct that are unrelated to a particular disciplinary action can also be considered in determining the penalty for a subsequent act of misconduct or a culminating incident.[7]

---

[6] [2003] 1 S.C.R. 66 (S.C.C.).
[7] *Calgary (City) v. A.T.U., Local 583* (1997), 61 L.A.C. (4th) 317 (Alta. Arb. Bd.).

Despite the foregoing principles, however, the arbitrator in *SKF Manufacturing of Canada Ltd. v. I.A.M., Local 901*[8] ruled that while prior acts of unrelated misconduct can be considered in determining the penalty for subsequent misconduct, those acts must have been documented in the employee's disciplinary record. The employee in this case was discharged for consuming alcohol at work, although his discipline records consisted of only three warnings that were unrelated to the alcohol incident. Relying on the warnings in the employee's disciplinary record and other incidents which were never formally recorded, the employer argued that this was a culminating incident for which dismissal was the appropriate penalty. The arbitrator reduced the discharge to a one-month suspension and ruled that it would be unfair to base the penalty on incidents for which the employee had not been formally disciplined; formal disciplinary measures informs an employee that further misconduct may result in dismissal and allows him or her to either correct the alleged conduct or challenge the allegations through the grievance process.

An exception to the rule that an employer cannot use prior non-disciplined misconduct to discipline or discharge an employee was established in *Air Canada v. C.A.L.E.A.*,[9] where a passenger agent was suspended for poor customer service following 13 prior non-disciplined incidents. The arbitrator reduced the suspension from 10 days to five, however, he stated that the employer can rely on non-disciplined matters that are not "stale", which combined with subsequent incidents demonstrate a pattern of carelessness or poor attitude merit discipline. The arbitrator held that some of the incidents taken together with the incident in question indicated a pattern of unacceptable performance warranting discipline.

In subsequent decisions more favourable to employees, arbitrators have recognized an additional exception to the general rule against considering previous non-disciplinary misconduct in a culminating incident. The ruling in *Newfoundland Light & Power Co. v. I.B.E.W., Local 1620*[10] established that incidents of misconduct can be considered in determining whether there are mitigating circumstances, such as an employee's good employment record, which might support a lesser penalty than the dismissal of an employee following a culminating incident.

The employee in this case was discharged due to employer concerns over his antagonistic and uncooperative attitude, his reluctance to follow safety procedures after having been spoken to about it on numerous occasions, violations of safety regulations, and a suspension following a viola-

---

[8] (1975), 9 L.A.C. (2d) 139 (Ont. Arb. Bd.).
[9] (1981), 4 L.A.C. (3d) 68 (Can. Arb. Bd.).
[10] (1990), 13 L.A.C. (4th) 341 (Nfld. Arb. Bd.).

tion, however, not all of these incidents were formally made part of a disciplinary record. The arbitrator held that the discharge must stand on those incidents which formed part of the formal disciplinary record, in accordance with provisions of the employee's collective agreement and with previous arbitral decisions.

The arbitrator also ruled that where an incident warranted the penalty of discharge, an arbitrator could consider an employee's good record in assessing things such as an employee's attitude, remorse and credibility and mitigating the penalty. While the arbitrator would not allow the employer to present prior incidents of the employee's non-disciplined misconduct to support its discharge penalty, the employer was permitted to provide such evidence to argue that mitigation of the discharge should not be ordered by the arbitrator.

3.5 CRIMINAL RECORDS

Third party access provisions in privacy legislation emphasize that employers can only access an employee's criminal record if the employee consents in writing, and employers must inform the employee of the type of criminal record information being sought. Once a pardon has been granted to an individual, however, employers receive no evidence that an employee's criminal record existed or that the employee was pardoned.[11] Human rights legislation prohibits against discrimination in employment on the grounds of conviction for a provincial offence or for an offence for which pardon has been granted.

In *MacNeil v. R.*,[12] the Federal Court ruled that placing criminal charges in an employee's personnel file does not constitute a breach of an employee's privacy, as defined by the *Privacy Act*. In addition to having a poor performance record, the officer had a criminal record in connection with assault charges involving a former girlfriend. The individual who had placed the criminal record in the officer's file did not intend to undermine the officer's re-engagement application with the RCMP or invade his personal privacy; he simply did not believe that the former employee had the potential to be rehired and determined that the employee would have had to disclose the criminal charges regardless of their placement in his file. Additionally, the Court ruled that the prohibition in the *Privacy Act* against disclosing personal information to third parties only applies to documents in the control of a government institution, and that criminal record documents do not belong to a government institution (or in this case, the RCMP).

---

[11] John Howard Society of Alberta, "Understanding Criminal Records", 2000.
[12] *Supra*, note 5.

4

Work Product & Professional Information

4.1 WORK PRODUCT

Following the decisions of the Supreme Court of Canada and the Privacy Commissioner of Canada, work product or tangible information resulting from an employee's work activity is not "personal information" as defined under privacy legislation. Work product is not information *about* an employee, rather, it is information *in association with* or *in relation to* an employee.[1]

A decision following a complaint filed with the Privacy Commissioner against IMS Health Canada indicates that little protection is afforded under *PIPEDA* to the work product of employees in the private sector.[2] The complainant here alleged that the company was selling information about the prescribing patterns of physicians without their consent. The information was gathered from Canadian pharmacies and comprised specifics such as the store number, drug identification number, drug name, form, strength, quantity, cost, doctor's first and last name, identification number, phone number, manufacturer, selling price, patient gender, and date of birth.

The Commissioner defined "personal information" as that information about an identifiable individual, meaning a natural person, which did not include legal persons such as corporations, partnerships or associations. The Commissioner held that a prescription in relation to an identified patient is personal health information about that patient, however, anonymized prescription information did not constitute personal information about the prescribing physician. Rather, a prescription is the outcome of professional interaction between the physician and patient and thus is more appropriately regarded as work product. With regard to the bodies covered by *PIPEDA*, the Commissioner stated that to interpret personal information so broadly as to include work products could allow for the inclusion of documents written by employees in the course of employment, reports prepared by

---

[1] Dagg v. Canada (Minister of Finance), [1997] 2 S.C.R. 403 (S.C.C.); Privacy

employees for managers' use, or legal opinions, and would therefore be inconsistent with the stated purpose of *PIPEDA*. Striking a proper balance involves determining whether the information is about the individual or is simply about the results of his or her work product.

Opponents of this decision argue that the work product of professionals should first be acknowledged as personal information belonging to them. Then a determination should be made as to whether its collection, use or disclosure is permitted by law, for example, in an instance where it may be in the public interest to disclose such information. The initial recognition of work product as an individual's personal information, realizing that it may not be afforded the same protection as other types of personal information, would allow for a balancing of interests between the holder's right to control the information and a body's right to collect, use and disclose the information. *PIPEDA* expressly excludes some, but not all, aspects of professional information, such as the employee's name, title, business address and business telephone number. Thus, if the drafters of the Act had intended to exclude an employee's work product or the manner in which an employee performs their job, they would have included this in the exclusion to the definition of "personal information". Instead, the drafters chose the broadest possible language to define personal information about an identifiable individual. The proper approach should be to recognize professional information as a subset of personal information under privacy legislation and then weigh any competing interests. If the law does not deal adequately with the collection, use or disclosure of such information, amendments should be made to the legislation in question, rather than removing all protections to which may attach to the information.[3]

Since the decision in IMS Health Canada, there appears to have been a shift in the Privacy Commissioner's thinking as to what specifically constitutes personal information in relation to the professional information derived from an employee at work. In subsequent decisions, the Privacy Commissioner has held that an employee's work performance and sales statistics comprised personal information, although the employees were deemed to have implicitly consented to the collection, use and disclosure of this information by willingly participating in a business environment where the practice of disclosing employees' personal sales results could reasonably be expected.[4]

Commissioner of Canada, October 2, 2001, Summary #15.
[2] Privacy Commissioner of Canada, *ibid.*
[3] Health Privacy in Canada, "The Professional Me Deserves Protection Too" by Kris Klein, Vol. 1 No. 4, August 2002.

In the public sector, the ruling in *Canada (Information Commissioner) v. Canada (Commissioner of the Royal Canadian Mounted Police)*[5] affirms that the *Privacy Act* affords no protection for the work product of public service employees. In this case, the Supreme Court of Canada held that the information about four RCMP officers sought by an individual who had commenced litigation against them was information that fell within the exemption of the general definition of "personal information" under section 3(j) of the *Privacy Act* with regard to an individual who is an officer or employee of a government institution that relates to the position or function of the individual. The litigant sought personal information *about* the officers under the *Access to Information Act*,[6] including a list of the officers' historical postings, their status and date, the list of ranks and when they achieved those ranks, their years of service, their anniversary dates of service, and any public complaints made against the officers. The RCMP refused the request on the basis that the records constituted "personal information" as defined under section 3 of the *Privacy Act*, and therefore were exempt from disclosure pursuant to section 19(1) of the *Access to Information Act*, which prohibits a head of a government institution from disclosing any record that contains personal information pursuant to section 3 of the *Privacy Act*. The Federal Court of Appeal held that only information regarding a public servant's current or most recent position had to be released.

On appeal to the Supreme Court of Canada, the Court ruled that the two Acts must be read jointly and harmoniously, and that neither takes precedence over the other. Although the officer's information did qualify as "personal information" pursuant to section 3 of the *Privacy Act*, the section 3(j) exception of the *Privacy Act* applied, allowing disclosure because the information was directly related to the general characteristics associated with the position or function of a federal employee. The information did not reveal anything about the competence of the officers or divulge any personal opinion given outside the course of employment so as to exempt it from disclosure, rather, it provided information relevant to understanding the functions performed by the officers. The Court held that the RCMP must disclose all of the information requested by the individual, and that the information applied retroactively and was not limited to an employee's most recent position.

Though the information sought was not work product *per se*, the Supreme Court's decision signals that any information related to the general characteristics associated with the position or function of a federal employee, including work product and certain information *about* a federal

---

[4] Privacy Commissioner of Canada, April 14, 2003, Summary #153; Privacy Commissioner of Canada, September 15, 2003, Summary #220.

employee, is exempt from the purview of the *Privacy Act* and does not constitute "personal information" pursuant to the *Access to Information Act*, thereby making work product accessible to the public.[7]

4.2 PROFESSIONAL INFORMATION

Jurisprudence establishes that not only is work product accessible to the public in accordance with access to information and privacy legislation, but so is certain work-related information. At issue in *Dagg v. Canada (Minister of Finance)*[8] was whether the information in logs signed by employees entering and exiting the workplace on weekends constituted "personal information" as defined by section 3 of the *Privacy Act*, and whether the information should be disclosed pursuant to section 19(2)(c) of the *Access to Information Act* and section 8(2)(m)(i) of the *Privacy Act*. Section 19(2)(c) of the *Access to Information Act* permits the head of a government institution to disclose any record requested under the Act that contains personal information if the disclosure is in accordance with section 8 of the *Privacy Act*. In turn, section 8(2)(m)(i) of the *Privacy Act* provides that personal information under the control of a government institution may be disclosed for any purpose where, in the opinion of the head of the institution, the public interest in disclosure clearly outweighs any invasion of privacy that could result from the disclosure.

The logs were kept by security personnel only for safety and security reasons. Dagg filed a request with the Department of Finance for copies of the logs for the purpose of presenting the information to the union to assist them in the collective bargaining process, hoping that the union would be inclined to retain his services. While the logs were disclosed, the names, identification numbers and signatures of the employees were deleted, thus, Dagg unsuccessfully filed a complaint with the Information Commissioner, arguing that the deleted information should be disclosed in accordance with the section 3(j)(iii) exception of the *Privacy Act,* which provides for the disclosure of information about a federal employee in relation to their position and functions including the classification, salary range, and responsibilities of the their position. While the Federal Court, Trial Division ruled that the information did not constitute personal information, this decision was reversed by the Federal Court of Appeal.

On appeal to the Supreme Court of Canada, the Court interpreted the *Privacy Act* and *Access to Information Act* together to determine that the number of hours spent at the workplace was information relating to the

---

[5] [2003] 1 S.C.R. 66 (S.C.C.).
[6] *Access to Information Act*, R.S.C. 1985, c. A-1, s. 4(1).

position of function of federal employees, as it allowed for assessment of the amount of work required for a particular employee's position or function. As such, the information did relate to the "responsibilities of the position held by the employee" pursuant to section 3(j)(iii) of the *Privacy Act* and was accessible to the applicant under *the Access to Information Act*.

A recent decision by the Assistant Privacy Commissioner of Canada indicates that an individual business e-mail address falls within the definition of "personal information" under section 2 of *PIPEDA*, and therefore may not be collected, used or disclosed by organizations without the individuals' knowledge and consent.

A University of Ottawa law professor received unsolicited commercial email at his business e-mail address from the Ottawa Renegades marketing season tickets, despite his having made an opt-out request. The team had collected his work e-mail address from the University of Ottawa website and his law firm website, and continued to send him e-mail without his consent, even after he indicated that he did not wish to be marketed further. Email addresses of staff were posted on the University Ottawa website to meet the university's expectation that employees be easily accessible.

The Assistant Commissioner held that section 4.3 in Schedule 1 of *PIPEDA* states that organizations may only collect and use personal information under section 7(1)(d) and section 7(2)(c.1) without the knowledge and consent of an individual if the information is publicly available in a professional or business directory, listing, or notice and is specified by the regulations. Further, such collection, use, disclosure must be conducted for the purpose for which the information appears in a directory, listing or notice. The Assistant Commissioner emphasized that *PIPEDA* defines "publicly available information" as an individual's name, title, business address and phone number; business e-mail addresses are not considered publicly available information since they are not specifically enumerated under the Act. Further, although the professor's personal information was publicly available, the purpose for which the Ottawa Renegades collected and used the email address was unrelated to the intent of the listing on U Ottawa website. It is believed that the intent of this decision is to protect individuals at work from spam and mass marketing that is not work-related.[9]

---

[7] *Supra*, note 5.

5

Personal Opinions in Employment

5.1 INTRODUCTION

In the employment context, individuals adopt views and form opinions in the course of their work and in regards to their colleagues, employees or employers on a regular basis. Once collected or divulged, issues may arise as to whom the information belongs to and what may legitimately be done with it pursuant to privacy legislation. In making their rulings on privacy and access to information issues, the Courts and Commissioners must frequently perform a balancing act between each party's interests, including the public's interest, to determine whose situation would be most adversely impacted by the decision.[1]

For the purposes of this chapter, the *Privacy Act* recognizes that the recorded personal opinions or views of public service employees are their personal information. However, an individual's views or opinions about *another* individual belong to that other individual, rather than to the one

---

[1] Jurisprudence also indicates that the personal opinions of union officials representing employees are protected as well by privacy legislation *vis-à-vis* the employer. In *Robertson v. Canada (Minister of Employment & Immigration)* (1987), 13 F.T.R. 120 (Fed. T.D.), an application by the Trenton Public Utilities Commission for a Canada Works Grant required the Commission to include a letter in its application from any union which represented their employees. After the application was denied, the Commission learned that the selected union had expressed opposition to the grant application. A Commissioner requested access to the letter under section 4(1) the *Access to Information Act* and was advised that certain parts of the information in the letter were exempt under the Act. The Commissioner filed a complaint with the Information Commissioner to argue for access to the severed portions of the record. The Information Commissioner informed the complainant that section 19(1) allowed a government institution to refuse to disclose any record containing personal information as defined under section 3 of the *Privacy Act*. An application for review of the Information Commissioner's decision was subsequently brought before the Federal Court. The Federal Court held that the official's general comments in the letter should be made public, however, the introduction of the term "personally" accompanying the impugned paragraphs clearly illustrated the author's own observations based on personal experiences and opinions, thereby constituting personal, confidential information which were properly withheld from disclosure.

holding those views or opinions. "Personal information" under the Act does not include a government officer's or employee's opinions or views given in the course of employment, or the opinions or views of individuals given in the course of performing services under contract for a government institution.

In the private sector, *PIPEDA* broadly defines personal information as information in any form about an identifiable individual, which may include the foregoing classifications in the *Privacy Act* but does not similarly enumerate specific examples. As the former Privacy Commissioner stated in a 2002 decision regarding a bank's refusal to allow a customer access to her credit score, "since *PIPEDA* is virtually limitless as to what can constitute 'information about an identifiable individual', its scope includes opinions. *PIPEDA*, after all, seeks to avoid limiting the definition of what personal information can be."[2]

The provisions of the *Privacy Act* and decisions pursuant to *PIPEDA* clearly emphasize that personal opinions given by employees in the course of employment or via work product do not constitute "personal information" of employees protected by the Acts. Like the *Privacy Act,* which considers the personal opinions or views of public servants about another individual to be personal information belonging to the *object,* rather than the *holder* of the opinion, *PIPEDA* has been construed by the Privacy Commissioner to prescribe corporate opinions about other individuals as personal information belonging to those individuals.

One distinguishing feature of *PIPEDA* is that in its present form, the Act is silent as to the manner in which an opinion about another individual may be held. The *Privacy Act* specifies that personal information in the form of opinions must be recorded, whereas *PIPEDA* simply refers to "personal information" as information about an identifiable individual, including opinions. This suggests that where an employee or employer has formulated an opinion about another individual without actually expressing

---

[2] Privacy Commission of Canada, February 27, 2002, Summary #39; This finding contradicts a prior decision in the *IMS Health Canada* case (see c. 4, **4.1 – Work Product**) suggesting that *PIPEDA* does in fact limit the scope of personal information. In that case, the Privacy Commissioner held that letters written by employees in the course of employment, reports prepared by employees for managers' use, and legal opinions (all of which arguably would comprise the personal opinions of employees), do not constitute "personal information" falling under the purview of *PIPEDA*. Thus, these decisions indicate an inconsistent interpretation and application of the definition of "personal information" in the handling of privacy complaints by the Privacy Commissioner, which may lead to confusion as to the actual scope of "information about an identifiable individual".

that opinion, the other individual may seek to be informed whether the employer or employee in fact holds an opinion about them and may be granted access to this information. The notion of a body being statutorily required to disclose an unexpressed opinion conjures up rather absurd and controversial scenarios, and does not necessarily guarantee the disclosure of accurate information. It also raises the question whether forcing the holder of an opinion about another person to divulge their thoughts may be invasive of the holder's personal privacy instead.

5.2 PERSONAL OPINIONS IN THE PUBLIC SECTOR

5.2.1 Opinions and Views viz. the Employer

The following case law illustrates the balancing act which decision-makers must carry out in considering the competing interests of employees and employers when privacy-related conflicts arise between these parties in the workplace. This process necessarily involves weighing an employee's rights to privacy at work against an employer's right to carry on business in an efficient and productive manner.

In *Lavigne v. Canada (Commissioner of Official Languages)*,[3] a federal public servant complained to the Commissioner that his rights regarding language of work, and employment and promotion opportunities had been violated. Employees of the Commission were interviewed by investigators and assured that the interviews would remain confidential pursuant to the *Official Languages Act*. The complainant requested access to the notes of the interview with his supervisor and to non-personal information in the investigators' interview notes. On the basis that disclosure could reasonably be expected to be injurious to the conduct of lawful investigations as per section 22(1)(b) of the *Privacy Act*, the Commissioner refused to disclose the information to the complainant.

The Supreme Court of Canada affirmed the Federal Court of Appeal's decision to order disclosure of the personal information, but not the non-personal information, in accordance with section 12(1) of the Act. Section 22(1)(b) could apply to future investigations, as well as those that were ongoing, however, the Court ruled that in this case, disclosure of the interview notes could not reasonably be expected to be injurious to the conduct of future investigations. The Commissioner had not established that it was reasonable to maintain confidentiality. His decision was based on the fact that the supervisor had not consented to disclosure of the information ac-

---

[3] [2002] 2 S.C.R. 773 (S.C.C.).

quired during his interview; however, he had not determined what risk of injury to investigations might be caused by the disclosure.

Decisions by Canadian information and privacy commissioners indicate that notes, comments, opinions or views made in relation to an employee's references are the personal information of the employee, unless that information was provided by the referee to the prospective employer in confidence.[4]

An employee for the City of Calgary applied for another employment opportunity with a different department of the City. The employee requested access to the reference notes created by the person conducting the interview, along with the names of the referees and the specific comments made by the referees. The department holding the job competition denied the request on the grounds that the two-page record contained confidential evaluations and opinions for the purpose of determining the candidate's suitability, eligibility or qualifications for employment, as defined by section 19(1) of the *Freedom of Information and Protection of Privacy Act*. The complainant subsequently asked the Information and Privacy Commissioner to review the department's decision to withhold access to the records.[5]

The Commissioner determined that the record containing third party opinions about the complainant's character and personality, as well as competence and skills in an employment situation comprised personal information belonging to the complainant. However, as the word "CONFIDENTIAL" appeared prominently on the record and as the interviewing party's affidavit stated that he believed that the discussion he had with the referee was implicitly confidential, the Commissioner held that the opinions of the referee had been provided in confidence and therefore, the content of the records came within the ambit of section 19(1) of the Act. Additionally, because the department had released 15 pages of records to the complainant, most of which had little or no severing, the Commissioner was satisfied that the department had properly exercised its discretion to not disclose the information.

A decision by the Information and Privacy Commissioner for Ontario indicates that notes taken by an employer during a meeting with an employee

---

[4] See Information and Privacy Commissioner for Ontario, May 20, 1993, Order M-132; Information and Privacy Commissioner for Ontario, October 18 1995, Investigation 195-045P; Information and Privacy Commissioner for Alberta, June 8, 1998, Order 98-008; *Inquiry Regarding Ministry of Social Development and Economic Security Records*, Information and Privacy Commissioner for British Columbia, October 5, 2000, Order 00-44.

[5] Information and Privacy Commissioner for Alberta, December 20, 2002, Order F2002-008.

which contain the opinions and views of that employee are personal information according to section 2(1)(e) of the *Freedom of Information and Protection of Privacy Act*. An employee at one of the detention centres of the Ministry of Community and Social Services complained to the Commissioner that the Ministry had improperly destroyed handwritten notes created by a human resources staff member during a meeting held to discuss correspondence from the employee about his concerns regarding the sexual identity group and workplace harassment at the detention centre. The notes were used to compose a memo which was later sent to the complainant with a copy also put on file.[6]

The complainant subsequently requested that corrections be made to the handwritten notes, maintaining that the notes comprised his personal information pursuant to section 2(1)(e) and (h) of the Act, but was informed that they had been destroyed after the memo was written. The complainant contended that this was a contravention of section 5(1) of Regulation 460 of the Act, which requires that personal information used by an institution must be retained by the institution for at least one year after use, unless the person to whom the information relates consents to its earlier disposal. The Ministry stated that keeping the notes was unnecessary as they were a duplicate of the information in the memo, however, the Commissioner held that the memo appeared to be a summary of the issues discussed at the meeting and concluded that notes likely contained more specific information than the memo itself and therefore the memo was not a duplicate. Further, the fact that the employee wanted corrections to be made to the notes but not to the memo suggested that the information contained in the notes was not the same as that produced in the memo.

The Commissioner agreed that the notes consisting of the employee's name and his views about sensitive issues met the definition of personal information under section 2(1)(e) and (h) of the Act, and since this information was used to prepare the memo and since the complainant did not consent to the disposal of the notes, the Ministry was required to retain the notes for the prescribed period of one year after writing the memo. Thus, the employee's personal information was not retained in accordance with section 5(1) of Regulation 460 of the Act.

Another complaint against the Ontario Ministry of Community and Social Services by a former employee of another government agency, which was funded and supervised by the Ministry, prompted an investigation of the Ministry's disclosure of information that had been provided by the former employee and some co-workers. During her employment with the

---

[6] Information and Privacy Commissioner for Ontario, October 18, 1995, Investigation I95-045P.

Agency, the complainant and co-workers had significant concerns about the Agency's operations and subsequently met with the Ministry to convey their concerns. The complainant asserted that the Ministry was aware of longstanding complaints about the Agency and encouraged her and her co-workers and ex-coworkers to state their concerns in writing, in order to assist the Ministry with its pending negative review of the Agency. The complainant and nine other employees agreed and wrote a letter to Ministry expressing their concerns adding their signatures to the letter.[7]

When the Ministry conducted its review of the Agency, it disclosed the letter to a member of the Agency's Board of Directors, who then attached the letter to the review and distributed copies of it to other members, Agency staff, other Agencies in the community, and to a local newspaper. The signatories' names were then published in the local newspaper. The complainant alleged that the signatories were later harassed at the Agency and that the Minister had to issue a "no harassment" directive to the Agency. She also alleged that the disclosure of the letter to the Agency eventually led to her dismissal and that of some of the other signatories to the letter. The complainant further contended that the contents of the letter were their personal information pursuant to section 2(1)(e) of the *Freedom of Information and Protection of Privacy Act*, which defines personal information as recorded information about an individual, including the personal opinions or views of the individual except if they relate another individual. Since neither she nor the other signatories consented to the Ministry's release of the letter to the Agency, the employee submitted that the disclosure of her personal information contravened their rights under section 42(c) of the Act, which states that an institution shall not disclose personal information in its custody or control except for the purpose for which it was obtained or compiled or for a consistent purpose.

The complainant maintained that she and the other signatories did not agree to sign a consent for the Ministry to disclose the letter to the Agency, and that none of them expected the contents to become public information in this manner. The Information and Privacy Commissioner determined that as the information in the letter contained the opinions and views of the complainant and other colleagues about the Agency's operations, it satisfied the definition of personal information under the Act. Further, the Commissioner held that the employees' concerns could have been brought to the attention of the Board without the disclosure of any names and that the Ministry should have severed the names from the review before its release. As such, the Ministry's disclosure of the complainant's name and opinion

---

[7] Information and Privacy Commissioner for Ontario, August 16, 1996, Investigation I96-016P.

was not for the same or consistent purpose for which it was obtained or compiled, and therefore was not disclosed in compliance with section 42(c) of the Act.

5.2.2 Opinions and Views viz. Colleagues

Privacy-related conflicts can also arise between colleagues over whose proprietary interests should prevail where information may be personal to more than one individual. This is particularly prevalent in instances where an employee is seeking to access personal information, such as opinions expressed about them by colleagues which might identify those colleagues. The case law is clear that colleagues' opinions about another employee belong to that employee; therefore, an employee's access rights to opinions expressed about him or her override the proprietary and confidentiality interests of those who offered the opinions.

At issue in *Canada (Information Commissioner) v. Canada (Minister of Citizenship & Immigration)*[8] was whether the names of employees interviewed, who had expressed personal opinions or views about their Director in the course of an administrative review, and portions of their interviews which would identify them constituted personal information that belonged to the employees or to the Director.

Allegations of discrimination and harassment by the Director of the Alberta Department of Citizen and Immigration Case Processing Centre prompted the Department to conduct an independent investigation of the corporate culture at the Centre. Employees, but not managers, who were interviewed were informed that their disclosures would be confidential and that notes taken by the Investigator would not be divulged to the Department. Following the review, the Director of the Centre was relieved of his duties and denied access to the interview notes. On complaining to the Information Commissioner of Canada, limited information was disclosed to him but the names of the employees interviewed and information regarding the position they held were excluded. Additionally, in keeping with section 3(i) of the *Privacy Act*, the views and opinions of the employees about the Director were severed from the report where the employees' identity would be indirectly revealed by the disclosure.

Interpreting the *Access to Information Act* and the *Privacy Act* together, the Federal Court of Appeal undertook to balance the privacy interests of the employees against the Director's access rights and the impact of the report on his career. The Court also considered the public interest in ensuring fairness in the conduct of administrative inquiries, which entails allowing

---

[8] [2003] 1 F.C. 219 (Fed. C.A.).

an individual the opportunity to be informed of unfavourable views against them, challenge their accuracy, and correct them if necessary. While both the employees and the Director had proprietary interests in the personal information in question, the Court determined that the promise of confidentiality made by the Department to the interviewees could not override the Director's statutory right to access the information and respond to their allegations. Without full disclosure and proper context, much of the information would be incomprehensible to the Director. The employees' interests in maintaining a good working relationship with the Director and avoiding legal action were minimal; they had no reason to fear full disclosure of the interview notes if their testimony was justified. Lastly, the Court dismissed the argument that disclosure might have a chilling effect on possible future investigations as one that has consistently been denied as a valid ground for refusing disclosure.

The case of *French v. Dalhousie University*[9] involved personal opinions of colleagues and students in relation to the department head of physiology and biophysics at the University of Dalhousie medical school. Colleagues and students ("authors") were asked to complete a survey and participate in interviews to evaluate the department head and make recommendations as to whether or not he should continue as head for another five-year term. The survey committee's report was critical of the department head and his management style and recommended a second term of only 18 months. The department head requested and was granted copies of the report by the Nova Scotia Supreme Court, and the University appealed this decision to the Court of Appeal.

The Court of Appeal, in determining whether the authors' submissions constituted personal information as defined by Nova Scotia's *Freedom of Information and Protection of Privacy Act*, upheld the lower court's decision that the views and opinions about the department head in the submissions were his personal information and not that of the authors, and should be disclosed. Such disclosure was not an unreasonable invasion of the authors' privacy on the basis that the overwhelming focus of the case was on the department head, the report caused him financial loss, and the authors' understanding regarding the confidentiality of the survey and their submissions diverged from that of the department head. The decision required disclosure of the opinions expressed about the department head, their assertions of fact as to his behaviour or action, and ancillary information necessary for his full understanding of the opinions and assertions, which included the authors' names and comments on the present or past operation of the school, the department or any part of it.

---

[9] (2003), 2003 CarswellNS 40, [2003] N.S.J. No. 44 (N.S. C.A.).

In *Board of School Trustees of School District No. 84 (Vancouver Island West)*,[10] an employee requested copies of records made pursuant to an investigation by the School District of the employee's complaint about a manager. The records contained the investigation report, a list of witnesses, the employee's submissions and interview notes, the manager's submissions and interview notes, and the investigator's rough notes of witness interviews.

The Information Commissioner held that any evidence of, or statements made by witnesses about the manager's workplace behaviour or actions (including any opinions or views expressed by them about the manager), the investigator's views or opinions, evidence given or statements made by the complainant and any findings or conclusions made by the investigator all constituted personal information of the manager according to section 22(3)(d) of British Columbia's *Freedom of Information and Protection of Privacy Act*. As such, disclosure of this information presumed an unreasonable invasion of personal privacy under the Act's provision. Therefore, the School District was required to withhold the manager's employment history, which included the statements made by witnesses and the observations of the investigator about the manager's workplace behaviour actions, as well as information that would identify witnesses who supplied, in confidence, personal information of the complainant and the manager. The School District was not required to withhold information that would identify the manager complained about or the complainant's allegations, or the investigator's findings that the allegations were not substantiated, since this was information about which the complainant was already aware.

5.2.3 Third Party Access to Opinions of Employer/Employees

Third party access to the personal opinions of employers or employees involves weighing the privacy rights of employees or employers against an individual's access to information rights. While the law favours disclosure generally, personal information such as an employee's employment history, job performance, competence and characteristics, and an employer's opinions and recommendations regarding the employee is beyond the scope of information which may be disclosed to third parties.

The decision in *Canada (Information Commissioner) v. Canada (Immigration & Refugee Board)*[11] involved balancing the privacy rights of

---

[10] Information & Privacy Commissioner for British Columbia, December 21, 2001, Order 01-53.
[11] (1997), 1997 CarswellNat 2436, [1997] F.C.J. No. 1812 (Fed. T.D.).

5.2.3 PRIVACY IN EMPLOYMENT

Board employees against an individuals' access to information rights, as well as the public interest in ensuring the integrity of future investigations. Following the publication of two articles in a Vancouver newspaper, which apparently were based on incidents that occurred during in camera hearings at the Refugee Division of the Immigration and Refugee Board, the Chairperson of the Board ordered an independent investigation into the leak giving rise to the newspaper articles. The investigator was unable to determine who leaked the information and turned her notes and report over to the Board. Two requests for access to the information and two privacy requests for disclosure of compiled information were filed with the Board.

The Board decided not to disclose the notes and the report since the interviewees were promised by the investigator that their interview information would remain confidential. The Board also contended that labour relations compelled it to uphold the investigator's promise and that disclosing the information would hinder its ability to conduct similar investigations in the future. The Information and Privacy Commissioners argued that the report and notes should be disclosed as they did not contain information that was injurious to the conduct of lawful investigations in the future. In turn, the Federal Court granted the application for disclosure, stating that the Board did not have reasonable grounds to refuse to disclose the information. The investigator's promise to the employees interviewed could not override the obligation to release information under the *Access to Information Act* and the *Privacy Act*, which were designed to facilitate disclosure. The Court held that the board was not entitled to refuse disclosure to protect unspecified future investigations, and there was no evidence that disclosure would in fact impair future investigations.

The decision in *Canada (Information Commissioner) v. Canada (Solicitor General)*[12] established that certain opinions expressed about the training, personality, experience or competence of individual employees do not fall under the seciton 3(j) exception of the *Privacy Act*, which allows for the disclosure of personal opinions or views of individuals given in the course of employment as an officer or employee of a government institution. The Court ruled that section 3(j) should only apply when the information requested is sufficiently related to the general characteristics associated with the position or function held by a federal employee, and not when it concerns the competence and characteristics of an identifiable employee.

This case involved an application by the Information Commissioner for judicial review following the Solicitor General's refusal to disclose certain portions of a report on the Food Services Operations at the Regional Psychiatric Centre in Saskatoon, on the basis that the author's opinions and

---

[12] [1988] 3 F.C. 551 (Fed. T.D.).

the information which identified certain employees were protected from disclosure under the *Privacy Act* and the *Access to Information Act*. The report contained personal opinions of the author about specific employees and supervisors regarding their level of training and comparisons of their actual job function with the job descriptions which accompanied the positions. The Information Commissioner argued that the report itself was a publicly funded study by a public institution and ought to be available to the public.

However, the Court held that while the definition of personal information in the *Privacy Act* was deliberately broad and that contrary to the applicant's arguments, the effect of section 3(j) was not to create an exception to the general rule of privacy where government employees were concerned. There was no indication that qualitative evaluations of a government employee's performance were ever intended to be made public, and it would be unjust to consider an employee's job performance to be public information simply because the individual is employed by the government. The Court allowed the study to be disclosed on condition that the opinions related to the employees' training, personality, experience and competence were deleted.

At issue in *Dickie v. Nova Scotia (Department of Health)*[13] was whether a patient in a provincial treatment facility could access information relating to an investigation of a facility employee and the decision taken pursuant to the investigation. The patient complained that the employee had breached his professional duties by engaging in an emotional and sexual relationship with her. Following the investigation, the Department of Health informed her that no disciplinary action could be taken against the employee. The patient then applied for access to information in relation to the investigation and was granted access to much of the information, including names contained in the report, the employee's work-related conduct, and information communicated in confidence by other employees, as well as their names. The Department of Health appealed the Nova Scotia Supreme Court's decision.

The Nova Scotia Court of Appeal allowed the appeal in part, ruling that while the trial judge was correct in allowing the names to be disclosed, he erred in coming to this conclusion by limiting the definition of personal information instead of interpreting the language in a clear, broad and simple manner. The trial judge also erred in ruling that the employee's work-related conduct did not relate to employment history, which constitutes personal information protected by the *Freedom of Information and Protection of Privacy Act*. Further, the Court held that the judge erred in finding that both

---

[13] (1999), 1999 CarswellNS 97, [1999] N.S.J. No. 116 (N.S. C.A.).

the employee and other employees did not communicate their information in confidence. The disclosure of employees' and management's opinions and recommendations regarding the employee, and his response to the allegations were presumed to be an unreasonable invasion of his personal privacy pursuant to the Act. The information was communicated in confidence and the balance did not tip in favour of disclosure. The Court concluded that the types of information which should be disclosed were the steps followed in the investigation, the names of employees who provided statements, communications by the patient to them regarding her allegations, and the decision made in relation to the employee over the allegations.

In the *Board of School Trustees of School District No. 44 (North Vancouver)*,[14] a parent applied for access to a letter sent by a secondary school principal to a teacher and coach of a school sports team, regarding the coach's decision to dismiss the complainant's daughter from the tryouts for the team. The letter was sent to the coach following an informal investigation of the parent's allegations that the coach had unfairly and arbitrarily cut the daughter from the team tryouts, instructing the coach to reinstate the daughter on a trial basis. The school board initially refused to disclose the letter, but subsequently did so in severed form on the grounds that disclosure would unreasonably invade the coach's privacy regarding her employment history and personal evaluations, pursuant to section 22(2)(d) and (g) of the *Freedom of Information and Protection of Privacy Act*.

The withheld information in full comprised evaluations consisting of the investigators' interpretations and opinion of the coach and the facts surrounding the daughter's dismissal from the team tryouts, their conclusions of the investigation, information regarding the personnel record, and the principal's instructions to the coach. The Information Commissioner held that the information consisted of the coach's personal information within the meaning of the Act, disclosure of which would presume an unreasonable invasion of personal privacy. The Commissioner further determined that the withheld information would not provide additional insight into the school board's investigation or resolution of the complaint and was not necessary to show that the board carried out its obligations of procedural fairness.

5.3 PERSONAL OPINIONS IN THE PRIVATE SECTOR

Under the purview of *PIPEDA*, personal opinions of an employee given in the course of their employment are not considered personal information

---

[14] Information & Privacy Commissioner for British Columbia, August 10, 2001, Order 00-38.

about or belonging to that employee, and therefore are not protected from disclosure. Likewise, corporate opinions in relation to another individual constitute personal information about and belonging to that individual and must be disclosed to them upon an access to information request.

A complaint filed with the Privacy Commissioner against IMS Health Canada alleged that the company was selling information about the prescribing patterns of physicians without their consent. The information was gathered from Canadian pharmacies and comprised specifics such as the store number, drug identification number, drug name, form, strength, quantity, cost, doctor's first and last name, identification number, phone number, manufacturer, selling price, patient gender, and date of birth.

The Commissioner defined "personal information" as that information about an identifiable individual, not including legal persons such as corporations, partnerships or associations. The Commissioner held that a prescription in relation to an identified patient is personal health information about that patient, however, anonymized prescription information did not constitute personal information about the prescribing physician. Rather, a prescription is the outcome of professional interaction between the physician and patient and thus, is more appropriately regarded as work product. With regard to the bodies covered by *PIPEDA*, the Commissioner stated that:

> To interpret personal information so broadly as to include work products could allow for the inclusion of documents written by employees in the course of employment, reports prepared by employees for managers' use, or legal opinions, and would therefore be inconsistent with the stated purpose of *PIPEDA*.[15]

The implication of this decision is that personal opinions of employees or professionals given in the course of their employment are not viewed as personal information about or belonging to the employee as defined by the Act and therefore is afforded no legal protection.

A later decision by the Privacy Commission held that a corporate opinion in relation to another individual, specifically a bank customer, constituted personal information about and belonging to the customer and therefore was subject to protection under *PIPEDA*.

In this case, the individual complained over the bank's refusal to disclose her credit score to her following the denial of her application for a mortgage. The portion of the score that the bank would not release incorporated factors specific to the institution in calculating an internal credit score according to a credit scoring model developed by the bank. The bank

---

[15] Privacy Commissioner of Canada, October 2, 2001, Summary #15.

argued that an internal credit score is not personal information coming within the ambit of *PIPEDA* as it is not collected but rather internally generated, and that an internal credit score cannot be released as it would reveal confidential commercial information, specifically the scoring model, protected under section 9(3)(b) of *PIPEDA*. Additionally, the bank submitted that it was not required to disclose an internal credit score as the score is a corporate opinion or form of commercial speech which was protected under section 2(b) of the Charter.

Stating that the Act is virtually limitless regarding what can constitute information about an identifiable individual, the Privacy Commissioner held that any information about an individual, including the customer's credit score, whether collected, internally generated, or originating with the individual was "personal information" subject to *PIPEDA*. Further, given the Act's wide ambit, its scope also includes opinions about an identifiable individual, such as corporate opinions in relation to an individual's credit worthiness.

With regard to the bank's submission that its internal credit score constituted corporate opinion protected from disclosure by the freedom of speech provisions of the Charter, the Commissioner found the argument creative but unpersuasive. He held that by generating a credit score about the customer, the bank had already broken its right not to express an opinion and must not now be allowed to invoke Charter provisions to shield it against disclosing this opinion to the customer. However, the Commissioner accepted the bank's contention that the credit scoring model qualified as confidential commercial information under *PIPEDA*, based on the bank's substantial investment in the model, its genuine regard for the model as proprietary, confidential commercial information and its efforts to protect it as such.

6

Personal Searches of Employees

The majority of cases have held that while there is no common law right of employers to search employees, an employer may have an implied right to conduct searches.[1] For example, the right to conduct such a search may be found in the collective agreement, or may have effectively become a condition of employment by virtue of past practice.

In *U.A.W., Local 444 v. Chrysler Corp. of Canada*,[2] the employer asserted a right to perform a random personal search of an employee. The arbitrator expressly rejected Chrysler's assertion that there was a common law right of employers to search employees, but suggested that an implied right might be demonstrated "by reason of the size and nature of his company's operations" or because past practice had established such a right of search. It was held that this action was an invasion of the employee's privacy and without just cause. Of particular note to the arbitrator was the fact that the evidence did not disclose that theft of company property had been a major problem, nor did the company ever inform the union or employees that it claimed the right to conduct spot searches. The arbitrator also commented on the embarrassment an employee would naturally feel in being subjected to a spot check because of the suspicion of wrongdoing that might reasonably befall an employee so searched.

A search can only be justified either where the employer has a "real and substantial" suspicion of wrongdoing or pursuant to a clear provision in a collective agreement. Furthermore, where there are no express provisions permitting a search, the employer ought to be prepared to ask for police assistance if its request to look into personal effects is denied by the employee.[3]

---

[1] See *Monarch Fine Foods Co. v. Milk & Bread Drivers, Dairy Employees, Caterers & Allied Employees, Local 647* (1978), 20 L.A.C. (2d) 419 (Ont. Arb. Bd.) where it was stated at 421 of the decision:

> It is well established that persons do not by virtue of their status as employees lose their right to privacy and integrity of the person. An employer could not at common law assert any inherent right to search an employee or subject an employee to a physical examination without consent.

[2] (1961), 11 L.A.C. 152 (Ont. Arb. Bd.) [hereinafter *Chrysler*].

[3] *Amalgamated Electric Corp. (Markham) v. I.B.E.W., Local 1590* (1974), 6 L.A.C. (2d) 28 (Ont. Arb. Bd.) at 32 and 33.

In *Canada Post Corp. v. C.U.P.W.*,[4] the arbitrator rejected the corporation's argument that it had a general authority as an occupier of its premises to confer wide powers of search on its security officers. The arbitrator held that an employee can assert a right of personal privacy not only over his body but also over his clothing, including outer clothing, and those accessories which constitute the immediate personal effects of the employees. Simply put, it was held that there is a basic core of privacy for each individual employee and for his or her reasonable personal effects which the collective agreement did not permit the employer to invade.

In *Amalgamated Electric Corp. (Markham) v. I.B.E.W., Local 1590*,[5] the majority of the arbitration board relied upon *Chrysler, supra*, to find that "spot checks" of purses, parcels, and lunch pails constituted an excessive invasion of privacy. As in *Chrysler,* the company had not published a rule relating to searches or the inspection of personal effects and there had been no evidence of a pilferage problem to justify the search. In balancing the right to privacy over personal effects with the company's interest in the security of its own property, the board made the following statements:

> [P]reservation of the right of privacy with respect to personal effects ought to be jealously preserved. This right of privacy should not be invaded except where there are the clearest provisions in the . . . collective agreement to the contrary, except of course where there is a real and substantial suspicion that an individual is guilty of theft. In a case where theft is suspected and where there are no expressed provisions permitting a search, the company ought to be prepared to ask for police assistance if its request to look into personal effects is denied by the employee. The suspicion of theft should be based on sufficient grounds so as to justify this action.[6]

Where a right to conduct employee searches is not found in a collective agreement, an employer must demonstrate that employee theft constitutes an immediate threat to its interests.

In *Glenbow-Alberta Institute v. C.U.P.E., Local 1645*[7] the employer instituted a policy of checking the personal effects, including purses, of employees entering certain restricted areas of the museum. The union argued that this was an invasion of the employees' privacy. The arbitrator applied the "balancing of interests" approach to determine the "reasonableness" of the search and asked whether the employer must experience serious incidents of loss, damage, injury or death before additional searches can be

---

[4] (1990), 10 L.A.C. (4th) 393 (Can Arb. Bd.).
[5] *Supra* note 3.
[6] *Ibid.* at 32 and 33.
[7] (1988), 3 L.A.C. (4th) 127 (Alta. Arb. Bd.).

justified. In this instance, it was held that the employer was justified in conducting employee searches. The arbitrator noted that the museum had suffered losses for the past 10 years as a result of employee theft. The arbitrator also held that if the nature of the workplace is such that security is an unusually high concern, the employer may be able to take more intrusive search procedures than would otherwise be allowed.

Employers wishing to inspect an employee's locker also face a difficult justification test. First, the search must be based on a "real and substantial" suspicion of theft. Second, the inspection must be conducted in a fair and reasonable manner. Most importantly, with respect to the personal effects such as purses or lunch bags found in these lockers an employee has a clear right to privacy.

For example, in *University Hospital v. London & District Service Workers' Union, Local 220*[8] the issue was whether the employer had a right to inspect employees' lockers and the personal effects therein. Unlike the situation in *Chrysler* and *Amalgamated Electric Corp.*, the hospital had a significant pilferage problem which informal measures could not resolve. The search of the lockers was held to be justified on the basis of the management rights clause in the collective agreement and on the basis of an employee handbook which reserved the right to the employer to inspect lockers at any time. However, the employee was held to have a clear right to privacy with respect to his or her personal effects contained in the locker.

Any searches which are conducted should be done on a universal basis, so that all employees in a given work area are searched, or a selection process should be used which is random and does not appear to single out individual employees.[9]

Discipline may be imposed on employees for failing to comply with employer rules regarding searches. *Lumber & Sawmill Workers' Union, Local 2537 v. KVP Co.*[10] is the seminal case on the imposition of discipline for failure to adhere to these rules. This case established that the breach of a rule imposed unilaterally by the employer without the union's assent permits just cause for discipline only if the rule meets the following criteria:

1. It is consistent with the collective agreement;
2. It is reasonable;

---

[8] (1981), 28 L.A.C. (2d) 294 (Ont. Arb. Bd.).
[9] See *Lornex Mining Corp. v. U.S.W.A., Local 7619* (1983), 14 L.A.C. (3d) 169 (B.C. Arb. Bd.); see also *Drug Trading Co. & Druggists Corp. v. E.C.W.U., Local 11* (1988), 32 L.A.C. (3d) 443 (Ont. Arb. Bd.). See also *Progistix-Solutions Inc. v. C.E.P., Local 26* (2000), 89 L.A.C. (4th) 1 (Ont. Arb. Bd.).
[10] (1965), 16 L.A.C. 73.

3. It is clear and unequivocal;

4. It was brought to the attention of the affected employee(s) before the employer attempts to act on it;

5. Where the rule is invoked to justify discharge, the employee was notified that a breach of the rule could result in discharge;

6. The employer has enforced the rule consistently since its introduction.

In addition to requiring an employer to satisfy these requirements, arbitrators will also assess the reasonableness of the rule in question. Generally, for a rule to be found reasonable the employer must establish that it promotes health and safety in the workplace or advances a legitimate business interest.

With respect to employer search policies, the decision in *Progistix-Solutions Inc. v. C.E.P., Local 26*[11] summarized the law regarding such rules in relation to the discovery of a major theft ring. Employees had been required to undergo a parcel search as they left the warehouse where they worked, to which the union had not previously objected. Following the discovery of the theft ring, the employer mandated a search of the employees' outer clothing as well. Some employees were frisked, had their clothing searched while they were still wearing it, or were asked to lift their clothing to allow for a visual inspection of their waist band area, prompting the union to file a grievance of the clothing search. Prior to the hearing, the employer extended the search to all persons using the warehouse and amended the policy to provide for random clothing and parcel searches at the exit.

In assessing the reasonableness of the employer's search policy, the arbitrator balanced the employees' right to privacy against the employers' right to control theft problems in the workplace. The arbitrator ruled that the original clothing search policy was unreasonable as it had not first exhausted less intrusive measures to deal with its security problems, however, she upheld the policy in its revised form. To meet the reasonableness test, the employer was required to prove adequate cause for implementing the policy by demonstrating that it had exhausted other alternatives to searches, had taken reasonable steps to notify the union and employees, and had conducted the searches in a systematic and random manner. Only outer clothing was allowed to be searched after it had been removed from the body and body searches and visual inspections were held to be impermissible without a police officer present.

---

[11] *Progistix-Solutions, supra*, note 9.

7
Monitoring and Surveillance

7.1 E-MAIL MONITORING

7.1.1 Introduction

Email has been defined as,

> [a] document created or received on an electronic mail system including brief notes, more formal or substantive narrative documents, and any attachments. . .[or] any other electronic documents, which may be transmitted. . .[1]

A 1993 study indicated that 30 per cent of 1,000 firms surveyed searched their employees' computer files, electronic mail, and voice mail, subjecting more than 20 million employees to computer monitoring. Four years later, another study revealed that monitoring had increased 33 per cent with the result that 63 per cent of mid-sized to large firms reported that they conducted some form of electronic surveillance.[2]

More recently in 2001, the American Management Association found that more than three-quarters of U.S. firms now monitor their employees' phone calls, e-mails, Internet activities and computer files. The survey also indicated that 80 per cent of U.S. companies monitor employee e-mail and Internet use, a dramatic increase from the 35 per cent of companies in 1997.[3]

7.1.2 Reasons for Monitoring E-Mail

The growing use by employees of personal computers on the job, which are typically linked either to the Internet or to an internal network, has

---

[1] Erik C. Garcia, "E-mail and Privacy Rights" (1996) Computers and the Law, online: <http://wings.buffalo.edu/law/Complaw/CompLawPapers/garcia.html>.

[2] American Management Association, International Electronic Monitoring & Surveillance (1997 AMA Survey), online: <http://www.amanet.org/usindes.html>.

[3] Charles Morgan, "Monitoring Employee-Electronic Mail and Internet Use: Balancing Competing Rights", *Droit du commerce électronique*, Les Éditions Thémis, 2002 [*Morgan*].

allowed employers to have easy access to employee e-mail. Access to employee e-mail in order to monitor incoming and outgoing information is important for an employer for a variety of reasons.

> 1. **Limiting Recreational Use**: A key preventative factor is to eliminate time wasted by employees who engage in recreational activities while at work, such as playing computer-based games or surfing the World Wide Web.
>
> 2. **Network Security**: Monitoring e-mail is a technique which protects network security. The need to monitor e-mails arises because it can be used to download infected files which can compromise the security of an employer's computer network.
>
> 3. **Misappropriation of Company Resources**: Employee recreational use of the Internet can cause significant delays in Internet connections for legitimate business use especially when the employee uses the employer's network for transmitting large image files.
>
> 4. **Security**: Surveillance techniques are useful to monitor employee behaviour. For example, monitoring e-mail messages can reveal when employees engage in contractual relationships contrary to their employer's interests, when they compromise trade secrets, and when they publicize copyright-infringing and confidential material.
>
> 5. **Corporate Reputation**: Employers may implement computer monitoring to protect the company's reputation and good will. An employer may wish to defend itself against an employee who uses company e-mail and Internet access to visit sites and/ or send external e-mail messages which could tarnish the company's image.
>
> 6. **Legal Liability**: Finally, many employers are wary of employees utilizing corporate resources for actions which may incur legal liability such as sexual harassment, racial discrimination, trademark/ copyright infringements, defamation, trade libel, electronic harassment and corporate espionage.[4]

7.1.3 Legality of Monitoring

Many employers consider electronic mail sent and received using company computer equipment and stored on company computer networks to be the property of the employer. From the employer's perspective this is a business resource paid for by the employer and is to be used only for business purposes. Therefore, e-mail messages and telephone conversations

---

[4] James Noonan, Heather Devine and Riva Richard, "Using Computer Video Surveillance to Monitor Employees: Are the benefits worth the cost?" (*Employment Law Conference Paper*, McCarthy Tétrault, November 9, 1998) [unpublished].

made on behalf of the employee in the course of business should be made available for review for legitimate business and security reasons. For these reasons, an employee acting on behalf of their employer should have no reasonable expectation of privacy.[5]

An employee's perspective, on the other hand, is that e-mail is his or her private property, similar in nature to personal handwritten letters. Many employees believe that the password requirement means that others cannot access their e-mail and that the site is secure.[6]

However, courts and legislators in the United States and Canada have come to hold that the right of privacy is a "personality right" which is held by everyone and cannot be alienated. For this reason in part, therefore, it is inappropriate to suggest that ownership rights negate or subordinate privacy rights as the two kinds of rights are different and overlapping in nature, and are not mutually exclusive.[7]

In a recent decision, the French Supreme Court ruled on workplace e-mail privacy and concluded that employers do not have the right to access their employee's e-mail or other personal files.[8]

(a) American Approach

(i) Electronic Communications Privacy Act

In 1986, Congress enacted the *Electronic Communications Privacy Act ("ECPA")*. Before the enactment of the *ECPA,* federal law did not provide any guidelines for protecting electronic communications and moreover they were not protected by the constitutional right of privacy as defined by the United States Supreme Court.[9]

Pursuant to Title I, section 2511 of the *ECPA,* it is illegal for anyone to "intentionally intercept, endeavour to intercept, or procure any other person to intercept or to endeavour to intercept any . . . electronic communication".[10] While this section does not explicitly exclude the workplace from the scope of the Act, case law has substantially limited its applicability

---

[5] James Noonan, *et al., supra,* note 4.
[6] "Addressing the Hazards of the New Technology Workplace", 104 *Harvard Law Review* 1909.
[7] *Supra,* note 3.
[8] See *Nikon France v. Onos,* BNA's Electronic Commerce & Law Report (2001) <http://pubs.bna.com/ip/BNA/eip.nsf/id/a0a4u9d3a5>.
[9] Erik C. Garcia, *supra,* note 1 at 1.
[10] Title I, S. 2511 of Electronic Privacy Act of 1986, Pub. L. 89-508 (1996). This *Act* amended the *Federal Wire Tap Statute, 18 U.S.C.A.*

7.1.3(a)(i) PRIVACY IN EMPLOYMENT

to workplace monitoring of employee e-mail. For example, in *Steve Jackson Games Inc. v. United States Secret Service*,[11] and in *Wesely College v. Pitts*[12] the Court held that there can be no interception under Title I if the acquisition of the contents of electronic communication is not contemporaneous with their transmission. Because e-mail is often in transit for only a few seconds and most often acquired only once it has been stored, Title I rarely applies to the monitoring of e-mail.[13]

Furthermore the Act provides two exceptions which effectively allow an employer, who is the provider of the e-mail service, to access stored messages and other electronic communications irrespective of the nature (personal or professional) of the message regardless of whether the employee has consented to such monitoring.[14] Section 2511(2)(d) contains a consent exception, which provides that it is not unlawful so intercept the contents of electronic communications where the intercepting party has obtained consent from one of the parties to the communication. Section 2511(2)(a)(i) includes a business use exception, which allows an officer, employee or agent of a provider of wire, electronic wire, or electronic communication services to intercept, disclose or use that communication in the normal course of employment while engaged in any activity which is

---

[11] 36 F.3d 457 (5th Cir., 1994) cited in Charles Morgan, *Employer Monitoring of Employee E-Mail and Internet Use* (1999) [unpublished, archived at *McGill Law Journal*].

[12] 1974 F. Supp. 375 (D. Del., 1997) cited in Charles Morgan, *ibid*.

[13] See *Fraser v. Nationwide Mutual Ins. Co.*, Case No. 98-CV-6726 (E.D. Pa., 2001).

[14] Section 2511(2)(d) *ECPA* provides that it is not unlawful to intercept the contents of an electronic communication when the intercepting party has obtained the consent of one of the parties to the communication. Section 2511(2)(a)(i) ECPA provides a "business use exception" to the general prohibition of the interception of electronic communications. This exception applies where an officer, employee, or agent of a provider of wire or electronic wire or electronic communication services, "intercept[s], disclose[s], or use[s] that communication in the normal course of his employment while engaged in any activity which is necessarily incident to the rendition of his service or to the protection of the rights or property of the provider of that service. Thus, the exception will apply where the employer is the provider of the e-mail service and the activity occurs in the normal course of the individual's employment. Case law has held that any monitoring done by the employer is sufficiently related to its business interests to fall within the exception — see *Briggs v. American Air Filter Co.*, 630 F.2d 414 (5th Cir., 1980); *Watkins v. L.M. Berry & Co.*, 704 F.2d 577 (11th Cir., 1993) at 582-585.

necessarily incident to rendering service or protecting the property rights of the service provider.[15]

(ii) Common Law Tort of Invasion of Privacy

An employee may also bring an action against an employer who monitors e-mails for unreasonable intrusion into the seclusion of the employee. The key is that in order to be actionable, three elements must be present: there must be an "intrusion" which is "highly objectionable" to a "reasonable man". The U.S. courts have generally held electronic surveillance to be sufficient to establish the first element.[16] With respect to the second element, the courts examine the "degree of intrusion, the context, conduct and circumstances surrounding the intrusion, as well as the intruder's motives and objectives, the setting into which he intrudes, and the expectations of those whose privacy is invaded."[17] Lastly, the third element requires the court to find both that the employee had a subjective expectation of privacy and that the expectation was objectively reasonable. American jurisprudence suggests that an employee will have little success in bringing a claim against an employer on the basis of this tort in the context of employer monitoring of employee e-mail.[18]

Several American cases have addressed the issue of the employer's right to review e-mail messages. In *Smyth v. Pillsbury Co.*,[19] the Court upheld the termination of an at-will employee based on a review of e-mail transmitted over the company network. The Court stated the following:

> Again, we note that by intercepting such communications, the company is not, as in the case of urinalysis or personal property searches, requiring the employee to disclose any personal information about himself or invading the employee's person or personal effects. Moreover, the company's interest in preventing inappropriate and unprofessional comments or even illegal activity over its e-mail system outweighs any privacy interest the employee may have in those comments.

---

[15] Canadian Judicial Council, "Computer and E-mail Workplace Surveillance in Canada: The Shift from Reasonable Expectation of privacy to Reasonable Surveillance" by Michael Geist, March 2002.

[16] *Billings v. Atkinson*, 489 S.W.2d 858 (Tex., 1973); *Nader v. General Motors Corp.*, 255 N.E.2d 765 (N.Y., 1970).

[17] See *Crump v. Beckley Newspapers Inc.*, 320 S.E.2d 70 (W.VA., 1983) as cited in Charles Morgan, *supra*, note 11.

[18] See *Smythe v. Pillsbury Co.* cited in Charles Morgan, *supra*, note 11.

[19] 914 F. Supp. 97 (U.S. Dist. Ct. E.D. Penn., 1996).

A similar issue was addressed in a class action suit filed by employees of Epson American Inc. in *Flanagan v. Epson America Inc.*[20] In this case, Epson employees claimed damages based on the company's practice of reading employee e-mail. The action was dismissed as the Court found that the State (California) constitutional right to privacy did not protect employees from employer monitoring of e-mail in the workplace.

An e-mail policy was also at issue in *Bourke v. Nissan Motor Corp.*[21] The employer had read personal e-mail, including correspondence of a sexual nature, that had been sent out over the company's e-mail system. California's Second District Court of Appeal held that no privacy rights had been violated either under California's Constitution (which grants expansive privacy rights) or under common law. Critical to the court's decision was the employee's signing of a policy agreeing to restrict all use of company e-mail to company purposes. The policy also stated that by signing the policy, the employee was put on notice that e-mail would be monitored.

Likewise in *United States v. Simons*,[22] the court found no reasonable expectation of privacy where a systems manager traced visits to pornographic websites from an employee's computer and found more than a thousand pornographic files on the computer's hard drive. The court ruled that the search was not a violation of the employee's constitutional fourth amendment rights (the right of the people to be secure in their persons, houses, papers, and effects, against unreasonable searches and seizures), and that the employee had no reasonable expectation of privacy since the company had an Internet policy and a business interest in preventing unauthorized use of the Internet by employees.[23]

Similar results have emerged throughout the United States as it appears the Courts are ready to accept that employees do not have expectations of privacy if the employer is clear in removing any such expectation.[24]

(b) Canadian Approach

Under current Canadian law, employee surveillance in the private sector remains virtually unregulated. In the absence of a collective agreement that provides to the contrary, an employer may use electronic moni-

---

[20] (1990) SWC 112749.
[21] No. YC003979 (Cal. Sup. Ct., Los Angeles County, 1991).
[22] 29 F.Supp.2d 324 (E.D. Va., 1998).
[23] *Geist, supra*, note 15.
[24] See, for example, *Smyth v. Pillsbury Co.*, 914 F. Supp. 97 (U.S. Dist. Ct. E.D. Penn., 1996) and *Garrity v. John Hancock Mutual Life Insurance Co.* (U.S. Dist. Ct. (Mass.), May 7, 2002).

toring systems, overtly or covertly, to supervise its employees. The propriety of monitoring depends on the nature of the monitoring, the employee's awareness of the monitoring, the classification of the monitored activity as business or private and the egregiousness of the monitoring.[25]

(i) Criminal Code

Section 184 of the *Criminal Code*[26] was enacted to protect private communications only. The protection afforded by the Code is inherently limited by its terms and does not really affect an employer's right to access business communications paid for by the employer and made in the conduct of business. Essentially, it appears that section 184 does not protect electronic communication where the communication is not private, or if consent to intercept is obtained from at least one of the parties. A communication is only private if the parties to the communication have a reasonable expectation of privacy.

Like the U.S. *EPCA*, the *Criminal Code* includes consent and business use exceptions in section 184(2)(c), though the business use exception in Canada appears to be more limited in scope to those who are in the business of providing communication services. Section 342.1(1)(b) is the *Criminal Code's* anti-hacker provision, which makes it an offence for a person to fraudulently or *without colour of right* to intercept any communication to or from a computer by means of any device. This section may cover computer surveillance in the workplace, however, employers who believe in good faith that they have a right to monitor their employees may not be subject to section 342.1(1)(b).[27]

While Canadian courts have yet to apply *Criminal Code* provisions to the context of employer monitoring of employee e-mail, in light of these provisions it is very important for an employer to have a policy concerning the use of office equipment which clearly informs employees that telephone calls, voice mail, and e-mail may be monitored for legitimate business purposes. Such a policy, combined with the fact that the employer pays for telephone and e-mail services and expects these services to be used for business purposes, may defeat any expectation of privacy that an employee might have in his or her communications. Alternatively, the employer could implement a policy which makes it a condition of employment that the employee must consent to certain types of surveillance.

---

[25] Jeff Kray and Pamel Robertson, *Enhanced Monitoring of White Collar Employees: Should Employers Be Required to Disclose?* 15 Puget Sound L. Rev. p.144.
[26] R.S.C. 1985, C-46, as amended.
[27] *Geist, supra*, note 15.

(ii) Canadian Jurisprudence

There is no definitive Canadian ruling addressing the issue of employee e-mail. Who owns the e-mail in the context of e-mail sent or received by an employee via his or her employer's computer system is a question which has yet to be addressed by the Canadian judicial system or by statute. Depending on the approach one takes to this question, different legal arguments arise.

For instance, one view is that e-mail sent or received in this context is the property of the employer, to which an employee maintains no reasonable expectation of privacy. In other words, a search of an e-mail system is really a search of an employer's property.[28] The alternative approach is to view sent or received e-mail as the property of the employee. In other words, the assignment to an employee of an e-mail address is analogous to the assignment to an employee of a company locker. Thus, this approach acknowledges that employees have an expectation of privacy in their e-mail. This approach requires the application of the same legal criteria as would apply in cases of company searches of employees.[29]

Privacy legislation, jurisprudence and doctrine suggests that the issues require a balancing of employees' privacy rights against the employer's legitimate business interests; however, emerging case law indicates that employee privacy rights mitigate against the position that employers have an unfettered right to monitor employees' e-mail and Internet use.[30]

In *Pacific Northwest Herb Corp. v. Thompson*,[31] a former president had used the company computer at home for both work and personal use, including correspondence with his lawyer regarding lawsuit against the company for dismissal. Before returning the computer to his employer, he attempted to have everything pertaining to him removed from the computer hard drive, however, he later discovered that some of his correspondence was still on the hard drive. The employee subsequently filed a motion for an order for production of all documents that the employer might have retrieved from the computer, as well as an injunction restraining the employer from accessing or using the communications on the basis of solicitor-client privilege and right to privacy. The employee also sought an order that the contents of the documents be kept confidential by the employer.

---

[28] See, for example, Holly Rasky, "Can an Employer Search the Contents of Its Employee's E-Mail" (1998) 20 *Advocate's Quarterly* 221 at 221.
[29] See discussion of employee searches in section 2.5.2.
[30] *Geist, supra*, note 15.
[31] (1999), 1999 CarswellBC 2738, [1999] B.C.J. No. 2772 (B.C. S.C.).

The court granted an interlocutory injunction restraining the employer from accessing or using communications created by or sent to his solicitors and ordered the company to keep confidential the contents of any documents that it had retrieved since the disclosure by the employee was inadvertent and he had not waived his privilege. Despite the fact that the computer system belonged to the employer, the court ruled that the employee had a reasonable expectation of privacy in relation to documents created for his own family or personal use.

The decision in *Bell Canada v. C.T.E.A.*[32] indicates that it may be unreasonable to prohibit outright all personal use of email and the Internet in the workplace. This case involved the investigation and dismissal of an employee who had used email during business hours to forward pornographic and sexually explicit emails to colleagues and people outside the company. The arbitrator held that since the amount of time required to send and receive email is very short, this does not significantly infringe on the use of company time. Further, it is normal for employees to spend some of their time using the employer's equipment for personal reasons and even though the company had a code of ethics which did not allow for personal uses, personal use of email and the Internet did not amount to serious fault as do dishonesty and insubordination, unless the use is so frequent that the employee can no longer perform the duties under his or her employment contract. While the arbitrator agreed that some penalty was warranted, he ruled that the dismissal was not justified and ordered the employee's reinstatement.

On the other hand, a Quebec arbitrator has held that if the results of an investigation reveal an employee's abusive use of email and the Internet, the employer has grounds to dismiss the employee. In *Bell Canada c. S.C.E.P.*,[33] an employee was dismissed for misappropriation of company time and use of Internet against company policy. The employee was in a high enough position to determine his own overtime hours and as a result, accessed the Internet for personal use during his normal working hours and charged the employer with a large amount of overtime hours for performing his work duties after normal work hours. In fact, over a five-month period, the employee had spent 329 hours using the Internet to visit pornography sites during regular work hours, and had billed his employer for 120 hours of overtime in one month alone. The arbitrator concluded that the dismissal was justified because of the employee's flagrant misuse of the Internet

---

[32] (2000), 2000 CarswellNat 1389, [2000] R.J.D.T. 358 (Fed. T.D.), affirmed 2001 FCA 139 (Fed. C.A.).

[33] (2000), 2000 CarswellNat 3866 (Can. Arb. Bd.).

7.1.3(b)(ii) PRIVACY IN EMPLOYMENT

during normal work hours, and because of his failure to comply with the company Internet policy, which was neither abusive nor unjust.

Where an employer's right to monitor e-mail is provided for in a collective agreement, or where an employee has consented to e-mail monitoring, an absolute privilege to conduct such monitoring is created so long as the invasion of privacy does not exceed the scope of the consent.[34] The focus becomes one of reasonableness of the substance and implementation of a given workplace rule. Using this approach in relation to e-mail monitoring, the inquiry would focus on such factors as the notice given to the employee of the search policy, the clarity of the policy and/or the fairness of the administration of the policy."[35]

In *Bhamre Employment Insurance Claim Appeal*,[36] the appellant had been dismissed from his job at Imperial Oil Ltd. because of his personal use of work e-mail against company rules. The employer had access to these e-mails and stated that some of these e-mail messages could be considered sexist and racist, and were against the company's policy of a harassment-free work area. The Court found that Imperial Oil had a clear policy that its e-mail system was to be used for business purposes only and that the claimant was aware of this policy.

Even in situations where policies have not explicitly been made known to employees, it has been held that mere common sense should dictate that

---

[34] Where an employee has consented to e-mail monitoring, Canadian courts will examine the nature of the consent, whether express or implied, to determine whether it was validly and clearly obtained. Two Canadian cases have examined the issue of consent. In *R. v. Sanelli*, (sub nom. *R. v. Duarte*) [1990] 1 S.C.R. 30 (S.C.C.), the Supreme Court of Canada held that the fact that one party consented to monitoring does not remedy lack of consent by the second party to the communication; in *R. v. Cremascoli* (1979), (sub nom. *R. v. Goldman*) [1980] 1 S.C.R. 976 (S.C.C.) the Court held that the consent must be freely given.

[35] The approach taken by arbitrators when interpreting management's rights under a collective agreement is to contemplate various minimal restrictions to management prerogatives as summarized in *Lumber & Sawmill Workers' Union, Local 2537 v. KVP Co.* (1965), 16 L.A.C. 73 (Ont. Arb. Bd.). See Beth Wilson, "Search and Surveillance in the Workplace: An Arbitrator's Perspective" (1992) Labour Arbitration (Markam: Butterworths, 1992) at p.143. Often charter values are applied in making a determination that an employee's privacy rights have been violated. See *Doman Forest Products Ltd. v. I.W.A., Local 1-357* (1990), 13 L.A.C. (4th) 275 (B.C. Arb. Bd.).

[36] (September 23, 1998), CUB 42012A.

the promulgation of some material by email is not permitted. For example, in *Consumers Gas v. C.E.P.*[37] it was held:

> Lack of knowledge of the policy, however, in this case does not assist the grievor. Common sense should have prevailed, and suggested to the grievor that the cc mail system and the computer's storage system is not for her own extensive use and that the transmission and storage of sexual material would not be acceptable to the business. Common sense dictates that Linda Primiani's use of the computer went well beyond acceptable means. This case is similar to the *Insurance Corporation of British Columbia* (*supra*) case. Arbitrator Weiler found in determining what a reasonable employee would understand to be an appropriate use of the email, that the criteria would be whether the receiver or sender would want the message to be made public at the workplace. This is a basic common sense test, which in this case, the grievor did not pass.

In situations where the employer is bound to obey the Rights and Freedoms guaranteed in the Charter (e.g., a federal Department of the Government of Canada), some employees have argued that the employer's ability to monitor emails is a violation of section 8. This was the case in the Public Service Staff Relations Board case of *Briar v. Canada (Treasury Board)*.[38] In this case, several employees were disciplined after their employer, the Solicitor General of Canada–Correction Service, found emails sent and received by the employees that contained pornographic material.

The Relations Board extensively recited the various proper use policies the employer had in place as well as the various notices the employer sent to all employees. Then, while dismissing the employees' arguments that their section 8 rights were violated, the Relations Board says:

> In view of the employer's policy against the use of the email system for unacceptable purposes and a clear log-on warning that the system is monitored in accordance with such policies, it is difficult to see how, in these circumstances, the grievors can claim a privacy interest. Moreover, the employer's investigation was driven by a complaint on which it was bound to act. This is not a case of random surveillance. Nor is it comparable to urinalysis or personal property searches. These are email communications over which the grievors lost control once they pressed "Send". There are some 1,600 users on the [employer's] network.

It bears mentioning that in the Privacy Commissioner of Canada's Annual Report 2000-2001, the Privacy Commissioner expressed concern

---

[37] (1999), [1999] O.L.A.A. No. 649 (Ont. Arb. Bd.) at para. 71. See also, *Briar v. Canada (Treasury Board)*, 2003 PSSRB 3 (Can. P.S.S.R.B.).
[38] 2003 PSSRB 3 (Can. P.S.S.R.B.).

7.1.3(b)(ii) PRIVACY IN EMPLOYMENT

over employer policies which endorse wholesale surveillance of email or computer use, following a complaint by a Department of National Defence ("DND") employee. In this case, someone had gained access to the complainant's computer and downloaded email messages which contained personal information about the employee and derogatory comments about his colleagues. The messages were then printed and placed on the desks of several other employees, which prompted them to file a harassment complaint against the complainant. DND then hired a consultant to investigate the harassment complaints and provided him with the messages as evidence. The employee complained to the Privacy Commission, questioning whether his employer could use and disclose private email messages, which had been collected by improper means, in order to investigate the harassment complaints.

Because there was no evidence that managers or supervisors were responsible for accessing the employee's email, the Privacy Commissioner concluded that the employer had not contravened the *Privacy Act* and had not behaved unreasonably in the circumstances. Additionally, the employee's expectation of privacy was lost once the email messages had fallen into the hands of his colleagues, regardless of the rights or wrongs of how this occurred. However, although the Commissioner affirmed that employers must protect their employees against workplace harassment, this did not include unfettered access to employees' email:

> DND's specific policy on the Management of Electronic Mail states that there should be no expectation of privacy on the part of employees when using e-mail systems. I find this deeply troubling. The law on privacy has developed around the notion of the "reasonable expectation"; ... But I don't agree that it follows from this that an employee's, or anyone's, privacy can be simply eradicated by telling them not to expect any. While management has the right and the responsibility to manage, it has to operate within limits, including respect for fundamental rights. It is not for management alone to determine whether an expectation of privacy is reasonable.[39]

While there may not always be a reasonable expectation of privacy if an employee is using the employer's network and if the employee has been given notice of the relevant policies, the courts have held that where the employer is not the service provider of the e-mail system (i.e. the employee is using the Internet to exchange e-mails), there is a right to privacy in e-

---

[39] Office of the Privacy Commissioner of Canada, "Annual Report to Parliament 2000-2001", online: <http://www.privcom.gc.ca/information/ar/02_04_09_01_e.asp>.

mail. For example in *R. v. Weir*,[40] the Court found that an individual communicating on e-mail via the Internet has a reasonable expectation of privacy:

> In summary, I am satisfied e-mail via the Internet ought to carry a reasonable expectation of privacy. Because of the manner in which the technology is managed and repaired that degree of privacy is less than that of first class mail. Yet the vulnerability of e-mail requires legal procedures which will minimize invasion. I am satisfied that the current *Criminal Code* and *Charter of Rights* protections are adequate when applied in the e-mail environment.

7.1.4 E-Mail as Discovery Material

Anyone who files a lawsuit against a business can have access to all corporate e-mail if it is relevant to the litigation. Provincial and federal rules of procedure appear to include e-mail as a discoverable document, which may, therefore, be subject to subpoena.[41] E-mail messages are valuable discovery material because they are often written informally and can contain statements which would rarely be put into a written memorandum or document.

In *Reichmann v. Toronto Life Publishing Co.*,[42] the Court ordered that the files contained on a computer disk were discoverable as documents pursuant to the *Rules of Procedure*. Similarly, in *NRS Block Brothers Realty Ltd. v. Co-operators Development Corp.*,[43] the Court ordered the production of an internal electronic memorandum despite a claim that it was privileged as it was prepared in preparation of a potential settlement position.[44]

---

[40] (1998), 59 Alta. L.R. (3d) 319 (Alta. Q.B.), affirmed (2001), 156 C.C.C. (3d) 188 (Alta. C.A.). While this case is significant, its application to workplace monitoring is limited due to the fact that in *Weir* the accused's e-mail account was a personal one purchased from an Internet provider, rather than one supplied by an employer.

[41] For example Ontario *Rules of Civil Procedure*, R.R.O. 1990, Reg. 194, s. 30.01(a) a "document" is defined as including a "sound recording, videotape, film, photograph, chart, graph, map, plan, survey, book of account and information recorded or stored by means of *any device*" [emphasis added].

[42] (1988), 66 O.R. (2d) 65 (Ont. H.C.).

[43] (1994), 24 C.P.C. (3d) 132 (Sask Q.B.).

[44] See also *Merck & Co. v. Apotex Inc.*, [1996] 2 F.C. 223 (Fed. T.D.), affirmed (1996), 1996 CarswellNat 100, 1996 CarswellNat 1763 (Fed. C.A.), leave to appeal refused (1997), 1997 CarswellOnt 6337 (S.C.C.) where the Federal Court ordered the production of hard copies of electronic messages.

The case of *Nesbitt Burns Inc. v. Lange*[45] involved the use of email evidence to prove that the former vice-president and other former employees had misused the company voice mail and email systems to solicit clients by emailing them confidential and proprietary information. Nesbitt Burns produced this evidence as grounds to seek an interlocutory injunction to restrain the former employees from disclosing any information regarding its clients, and to restrain them from using the client information at their new workplace. Although the Ontario Superior Court admitted the email as evidence, it upheld the motion court judge's decision that Nesbitt Burns had not shown that irreparable harm would result if the injunctive relief were not granted. The Court held that monetary damages would be sufficient compensation for any loss sustained by the broker and dismissed its application for leave to appeal the motion court ruling.

Email was also used as evidence in *Lovelock v. DuPont Canada Inc.*[46] to successfully demonstrate an employee's fraudulent activity and argue dismissal with cause. The employer alleged that the employee had forged his supervisor's signature to approve the employee's expense account for a convention. The employee denied the forgery or that he had engaged in any kind of dishonesty. The company used its email records to show that emails sent by employee to his supervisor proved that the employee's explanation of the events leading to his dismissal did not make sense, were implausible and revealed that he was being dishonest.

On December 14, 2000, the Washington Court of Appeals ruled in the case of *Tiberino v. Spokane County*[47] that personal e-mail messages could not be discovered due to privacy concerns. In this case, the employee had been terminated for sending 467 personal e-mail messages over the course of 40 days, many of which contained vulgar language. After she filed a lawsuit for wrongful termination, representatives of the media sought disclosure of 3,805 pages of the e-mail messages being used by the employer to defend its decision. The Court ruled that access to the e-mails would not be granted.

7.1.5 Effect on Employees

Monitoring employee's use of e-mail may lead to employee psychological and physical health problems, increased boredom, high tension, extreme anxiety, depression, anger, severe fatigue, and musculoskeletal

---

[45] (2000), 2000 CarswellOnt 1296, [2000] O.J. No. 335 (Ont. S.C.J.).
[46] (1998), 1998 CarswellOnt 4626, [1998] O.J. No. 4971 (Ont. Gen. Div.).
[47] No. 18830-2-III (Wash. App. Div. 3).

problems. In *United States v. White*,[48] the Court summarized other concerns with respect to the effect of monitoring on employees:

> ... words would be measured a good deal more carefully and communication inhibited if one suspected his conversations were being transmitted and transcribed. Were third-party bugging a prevalent practice, it might well smother that spontaneity-reflected in frivolous, impetuous, sacrilegious, and defiant discourse-that liberates daily life.[49]

Additionally, others argue that as employee autonomy in the workplace is eroded by overly intrusive monitoring practices, so too may employees' inclination towards creativity and experimentation be curtailed. Unwarranted or overzealous monitoring may have a deleterious impact on working conditions:[50]

> When invasions of privacy occur, employees often feel that self-worth, morale, and the overall quality of working life are eroded. The ensuing negative impact of invasions of privacy on work quality and productivity is hidden human and real costs (for example, absenteeism and employee compensation claims), not often calculated by employers.[51]

7.1.6 Establishing an E-mail Policy

In light of the *Criminal Code* provisions and the direction provided by the small amount of judicial consideration of the issue, a company considering monitoring employee e-mail should first establish a policy in this respect. At a minimum, the policy should set out the following:

a. Purposes for which the e-mail system may be used;

b. Access to email on the part of third parties; and

c. Consequences of breaches of the e-mail policy.[52]

---

[48] (1970), 401 U.S. 745, at 787-89, cited in *Duarte, supra*, note 14 at 54.
[49] See also Laura Pincus Hartman, "The Rights and Wrongs of Workplace Snooping", *DePaul University*, online: <http://wwww.depaul.edu/ethics/monitor.html>. Research conducted by Swiss economist Bruno Frey found evidence that monitoring worsened employee morale and thereby negatively affected their performance. This was primarily the result of the employees feeling like the employer had low expectations of them because the firm felt the need to monitor.
[50] *Morgan, supra*, note 3.
[51] *Ibid.*
[52] Tom Wright, *Privacy Protection Principles for Electronic Mail Systems* (Ontario:

In developing these policies, attention must be placed on the purposes for which e-mail systems are used, the nature of the information exchanged via e-mail, the business of the organization and the technical limitations of e-mail systems. By informing employees that e-mail messages are subject to monitoring, an employee's expectation of privacy can be reduced or even extinguished.

In addition, a well-established and publicized policy of e-mail monitoring may be the basis for a finding of implied consent, and exempt the employer from liability pursuant to section 184 of the *Criminal Code*. Alternatively, employers may consider requiring employees to consent to monitoring as a term of their employment. If possible, such a policy should be made part of the terms and conditions of employment at the time of hire. Otherwise, signed acknowledgements may be obtained from employees indicating they understand the policy and consent to monitoring.

7.2 VIDEO SURVEILLANCE

7.2.1 Introduction

The widespread use of video surveillance in workplaces raises fundamental questions related to the employee's right to privacy. The information and images that can be captured by video surveillance, such as a person's physical characteristics, voice, speech and mannerisms, are unique and highly personal.[53] The systematic observations of employees, regardless of any involvement in wrongdoing, is a *prima facie* invasion of privacy. The advent of private sector privacy legislation such as the federal *Personal Information Protection and Electronic Documents Act* is now a further consideration that must be examined when looking at the propriety of video surveillance.

7.2.2 Reasons Cited for Using Video Surveillance

Employers justify implementing surveillance for the following reasons:

1. To prevent theft or the general misappropriation of company resources, and as a protection mechanism against fraud.

Information and Privacy Commissioner, February 1994) at 15, online: <http://www.ipc.on.ca>.

[53] New South Wales Privacy Committee, "Inquiry into Video Surveillance in the Workplace," c. 3.1 online: <http://www.austlii.edu.au/au/other/privacy/video/31.html>.

2. To enable an employer to document employee actions over a period of time (for example in cases where employee behaviour is difficult to intercept), and also to document misconduct such as sexual harassment and aggression.[54]
3. To ensure employees conform to required health and safety standards and regulations.
4. In the financial service industry (i.e. banks, brokerages, insurance firms, realtors) employers have a special interest in monitoring activities to ensure compliance with federal and local laws.

7.2.3 Video Surveillance in the Workplace

The legitimacy of the use of video surveillance in the workplace depends on whether there are compelling circumstances to justify such action. An employer must be able to demonstrate a substantial interest which requires protecting through this medium. The installation of video cameras in particular areas will only be permitted if it can be shown that there is an imminent threat in that workplace area of theft or other kinds of crime.[55] It is a matter of balancing competing considerations after recognizing that any use of cameras to observe employees at work is intrinsically objectionable to the person being observed.[56] The degree of objection depends on the way the cameras are deployed and the purpose for which they are used, ranging

---

[54] For example, in the case of *Richardson v. Davis Wire Industries Ltd.* (1997), 28 C.C.E.L. (2d) 101 (B.C. S.C.) at 114: video surveillance was used successfully by an employer to dismiss a long-term employee who was sleeping during his night shift. Justice Kirkpatrick of the British Columbia Supreme Court held that a videotape of an employee engaged in wrongdoing was admissible as evidence in a wrongful dismissal hearing:

In my view, if the videotape evidence is probative of a matter in issue, and is made in the context of the company's legitimate right to investigate Mr. Richardson's misconduct, then it ought to be admitted.

[55] Gordon F. Luborsky and John C. O'Reilly, *Employee Surveillance: Defining the Boundaries* (Toronto: Thomson Canada Limited, 1997) at 15.

[56] In a recent case before the Ontario Superior Court of Justice, Clayton Ruby attempted to obtain an order prohibiting the use as evidence of a surveillance camera videotape catching his client allegedly stealing computer equipment from a police station anteroom. In support of his argument that people visiting this room had a reasonable expectation of privacy, Mr. Ruby used footage of a sexual encounter caught on tape by the same camera. He then posed this question to Humphrey J.: "Why would the trysting couple have chosen the room for a sexual encounter if it were not a spot everyone understood to be private?"

7.2.3 PRIVACY IN EMPLOYMENT

from unacceptable in the case of constant surveillance of conduct and work performance to non-objectionable in the case of short-term individual application for training purposes.

Video cameras cannot be used to intimidate[57] nor can they be used unless there is a real and substantial suspicion of wrongdoing and they are used in a reasonable manner.[58] Furthermore, there must be a direct relationship between the use of the video camera and the likelihood that it will address the employer's concerns.[59]

In *Puretex Knitting Co. v. C.T.C.U.*,[60] the employer had installed cameras in work areas for the said purpose of deterring theft. The union, however, argued that the cameras were installed for the purpose of spying on employees and this constituted an abuse of management rights. While it was likely that the surveillance was within the company's management rights, the arbitrator, upon a review of American jurisprudence on this issue, ordered the cameras removed despite his statement that the surveillance was likely within the company's management rights. It was held that the use of video surveillance which would constantly monitor the work performance and conduct of employees was "seriously offensive in human terms". After analysis, only the cameras located in the parking lot, loading dock area and storage areas were allowed to remain.[61]

---

[57] See *K-Mart Canada Ltd. v. S.E.I.U., Local 183* (1981), (sub nom. *S.E.I.U., Local 183 v. K-Mart Canada Ltd.*) 81 C.L.L.C. 16,084 (Ont. L.R.B.), where it was held that:

> In this case the Board must first consider the impact of the open and continuous surveillance of two employees who were the spearhead of the union organizing campaign. Spying on employees is not new to the catalogue of unfair labour practices resorted to by employers who are extreme in their determination to stop their employees from exercising their collective bargaining rights. This Board has previously found instances of covert surveillance to be unlawful interference with the rights of employees under the Act; (see, for example, *Tandy Electronics Ltd. v. U.S.W.A.*, [1979] O.L.R.B. Rep. 248 (Ont. L.R.B.), affirmed (1979), 79 C.L.L.C. 14,216 (Ont. Div. Ct.)). In its very first reported decision the National Labour Relations Board was confronted with the tactic of surveillance as a method of discouraging union activity. From that time to the present, with the endorsement of the Courts, the NLRB has consistently found surveillance or the attempt to create the impression of surveillance of union activity to be unlawful interference with the rights of union association expressly protected by law.

[58] *Labatt, infra*, note 71.
[59] *Ibid.*
[60] (1979), 23 L.A.C. (2d) 14 (Ont. Arb. Bd.).
[61] In *Lenworth Metal Products Ltd. v. U.S.W.A., Local 3950* (2000), 2000

MONITORING AND SURVEILLANCE   7.2.3

In *U.A.W., Local 707 v. Ford Motor Co. of Canada*[62] the union objected to the company's use of closed circuit television as part of a remote control system at certain gates of a manufacturing plant. There was no issue of surveillance in this case, rather the cameras simply upset the employees. In actuality, the cameras were installed to enable guards located at other gates to identify those employees seeking entrance through gates where guards were no longer on duty and thereby facilitate the employee's entrance. The arbitrator dismissed the grievance, finding that there had been no change in rules or regulations, rather only a change in the technique of implementing those rules. The new techniques were found not to violate the collective agreement or invade the privacy of the employees.

With the coming into force of the federal *Personal Information Protection and Electronic Documents Act*,[63] we are beginning to see the Privacy Commissioner of Canada issue his findings on the propriety of employers using video surveillance in the workplace.

In one such case,[64] the Commissioner investigated the use of video cameras set up by the employer in order to reduce vandalism and theft. The employer had no intention on monitoring its employees with the camera, and, in fact, when it was discovered that the camera was pointed in a direction that picked up images of the employees, the employer changed the camera's position.

The cameras could rotate and zoom in but they did not record. Notwithstanding that there was no recording, the Commissioner went on to examine if the use of the camera violated section 5(3) of the Act. That section states that an organization may collect, use or disclose personal information only for purposes that a reasonable person would consider are appropriate in the circumstances. In determining the reasonableness of the use, the Commissioner considered the following questions:

(1) Is the measure demonstrably necessary to meet a specific need?

(2) Is it likely to be effective in meeting that need?

(3) Is the loss of privacy proportional to the benefit gained?

(4) Is there a less privacy-invasive way of achieving the same end?

CarswellOnt 4282 (Ont. Div. Ct.), the court decided that the arbitrator's decision to permit non-operational video cameras in the workplace during working hours for internal safety purposes was not "patently unreasonable".

[62] (1971), 23 L.A.C. 96 (Ont. Arb. Bd.).
[63] See Chapter 4.
[64] Reported on the Commissioner's website (www.privcom.gc.ca) as *PIPED Act Case Summary #114*.

7.2.3 PRIVACY IN EMPLOYMENT

In this case, the Commissioner found that the company failed to prove that the incidents of vandalism were sufficiently serious as to affirmatively answer the first question. Further, the Commissioner questioned the effectiveness of the cameras in deterring the illegal activity and, at the same time, noted that employees may get the perception that their comings and goings were being watched, even if that was not objectively the case. Finally, the Commissioner noted that there were less privacy invasive solutions available, such as installing better lighting. For all those reasons, the Commissioner found that the company's use of this type of video surveillance was in contravention of section 5(3) of the Act and recommended that the company remove the cameras.

As an additional note, the Commissioner also expressed his view that had the company used any information gained through the use of the cameras as part of any disciplinary action against an employee, the Commissioner would have strongly interpreted such use as inappropriate.

While it is impossible to be completely certain, this matter addressed by the Commissioner appears to have been challenged in the Federal Court in *Eastmond v. Canadian Pacific Railway*.[65] The Court ultimately made several findings of fact that were different than the Commissioner (because the evidence before the Court was different than that before the Commissioner), and ultimately the Court came to a different conclusion.

Importantly, the Court noted that the issue of an employer using video surveillance is something that can give rise to the application of *PIPEDA* and thus can result in the Privacy Commissioner and, ultimately, the Federal Court in having the jurisdiction to evaluate the correctness of such use.[66]

The Court was prepared to adopt the test applied by the Commissioner (referred to above) and thus first had to determine if the use of the video surveillance was reasonable. In doing so, the Court also agreed to take into account the four-part test developed by the Commissioner when he was tasked into looking into the reasonableness of the use of the surveillance. While emphasizing that this necessarily was a very contextual and fact specific type of analysis, the Court, with the aid of established arbitral jurisprudence in the area, came to the conclusion that a reasonable person would consider the purposes of the video surveillance to be appropriate. Specifically, the Court noted the following in support of this conclusion:

---

[65] 2004 FC 852, 2004 CarswellNat 1842 (F.C.).
[66] Contrast with *L'Ecuyer c. Aéroports de Montréal*, 2003 FCT 573, 2003 CarswellNat 1286, 2003 CarswellNat 2621 (Fed. T.D.), affirmed 2004 CarswellNat 4173, 2004 CAF 237 (F.C.A.).

MONITORING AND SURVEILLANCE 7.2.3

> The collection of personal information is not surreptitious - warning signs are displayed. The collection of personal information is not continuous - it is brief, capturing only a person's image when that person is within the footprint of the camera. The collection is not limited to CP employees - it captures the images of contractors, visitors, suppliers and trespassers. The collection is not to measure a CP employee's work performance and while it is true a camera may occasionally capture a CP employee at work outside the shops, CP could not use those images to measure that employee's productivity because such a use of the information would be a use for a purpose other than that which prompted its collection as a security measure. More importantly, the recorded images are kept under lock and key and the recordings are only accessed by responsible managers and CP police if there is an incident reported. If there are no incidents recorded which require investigations, the recordings are destroyed within an appropriate time frame. The evidence satisfies me CP has established a legitimate need to have the cameras installed where they were and to record those persons who would pass its fixed footprints. While the cross-examination of CP deponents established, in some cases, a lack of correlation between camera location and incidents and, in other cases, between cause of loss, I am satisfied, on the whole of the evidence, CP identified numerous past incidents which justify the need to have surveillance cameras in place.[67]

Furthermore, the Court found that the use of the cameras would meet the employer's needs because the cameras were an effective deterrent and the purpose of the surveillance was to stop wrongdoing. Lastly, the Court found that the loss of privacy was minimal and said:

> Indeed, if there were no recorded incidents, it means none of the images captured by the cameras were viewed. The Privacy Commissioner was of the view a person whose images might be recorded had a low expectation of privacy because the cameras were located to capture personal information in locations which were public places. I share his assessment. Generally, such a view accords with the thrust of the cases decided by the Supreme Court of Canada in section 8 Charter cases where an analysis of a reasonable expectation of privacy is weighed.
>
> On this point, it must be remembered the recordings are never viewed unless an incident requiring an investigation occurs. This factor, coupled with my findings of how and what the cameras capture, lead me to conclude the loss of privacy is proportional to the benefit gained from their collection.[68]

---

[67] *Eastmond, supra*, note 65 at paras. 176-177.
[68] *Ibid.*, at paras. 180-181.

7.2.3 PRIVACY IN EMPLOYMENT

On the last part of the test (*i.e.*, whether there was a less privacy-invasive way of achieving the desired purpose), the Court was satisfied that the employer looked at alternatives such as installing fences and hiring additional security guards and weighed them in the context of its operations.

Having found that the purposes were reasonably appropriate to warrant video surveillance, the Court then went on to consider if the PIPEDA consent requirements were met. Interestingly, the Court concludes on this point that the collection of the person's information only takes place when the employer views the recording to investigate an incident of wrongdoing. Then the Court assumes that if the recording captured a wrongdoing, asking the wrongdoer's permission would compromise the availability of the information for the purpose of the investigation. That being the case, the exception to PIPEDA's general requirement that consent be obtained was available to the employer.

In a recent decision by the Assistant Privacy Commissioner of Canada, the Assistant Commissioner determined that a company's video surveillance of workstations of employees was unreasonable pursuant to the four-step test.[69] The Canadian Food Inspection Agency (CFIA) employee worked as a "Veterinarian in Charge" at a federally registered meat processing plant and complained that the company was collecting his personal information by video surveillance without his consent. The plant manager had installed the video cameras without consulting the CFIA or establishing related policies and procedures. The cameras were motion activated but did not have pan or zoom capabilities, and images were recorded onto the hard drive. The company claimed to use video surveillance to monitor hygiene and safety, and address security concerns, despite the fact that CFIA inspectors and a Veterinarian in Charge were always on site, and that the cameras were not focused on workstations at other federal facilities. Further, while the complainant was told that the cameras would not be used to observe him when they were initially installed, there were documented examples of instances where the company had disclosed the employee's personal information to his supervisor at the CFIA. However, the videotaping of employees at personal workstations had ceased after *PIPEDA* was enacted on January 1, 2001; therefore, any violation of their privacy prior to *PIPEDA* was outside the Assistant Privacy Commissioner's jurisdiction.

The Assistant Privacy Commissioner held that no evidence was provided to support that the surveillance was important for monitoring food safety, particularly when the individuals responsible for monitoring food safety worked on site. The use of video surveillance did not appear to be demonstrably necessary or useful to ensuring food safety, and the focus of

---

[69] Privacy Commissioner of Canada, January 27, 2005, Summary #290.

the cameras on the CFIA inspectors' workstations without their consent clearly constituted an invasion of their privacy. The Assistant Privacy Commissioner recommended that the company remove the cameras from the area where the inspectors' workstations were located and warned the company that it could only use personal information that it deliberately collected without employee consent pursuant to section 7(2)(a) and (b) of *PIPEDA*, specifically, if consent could not be obtained in a timely way or if the employees' knowledge, or consent of such collection would compromise the availability or the accuracy of the information and the collection is reasonable for purposes related to investigating a breach of an agreement or contravention of a Canadian law.

7.2.4 Video Surveillance outside the Workplace

Employers engage in video surveillance of employees outside of the workplace because of concerns that employee absences are not due to legitimate illnesses or injuries. Employers are also generally skeptical with respect to the medical profession's ability to diagnose the actual extent of an employee's alleged disability. These concerns, coupled with the fact that employee absences cause the employer to incur great costs in long term disability and workers compensation premiums, are the impetus behind video surveillance outside of the workplace.

However, certain conditions must be met before an arbitrator will accept video surveillance evidence of an employee engaging in activities inconsistent with their alleged disability. In deciding whether to admit video surveillance evidence, the privacy rights of the employee must be balanced against the employer's right to investigate potential abuses of employment benefits.

In *Alberta Wheat Pool v. Grain Workers' Union, Local 333*[70] the arbitrator held that:

> [C]onducting surveillance on an employee and videotaping his or her conduct without knowledge or consent will amount to a breach of the employee's right to privacy, unless such intrusive conduct can be demonstrably justified by the employer. The onus of establishing that justification rests with the employer.
>
> In the course of that investigation, however, before the employer goes so far as to intrude on the right to an employee's privacy, it must be able to justify that such a course is the only one open to it and the only way in which the truth can be ascertained.

---

[70] (1995), 48 L.A.C. (4th) 332 (B.C. Arb. Bd.) at 341.

7.2.4 PRIVACY IN EMPLOYMENT

In making a determination as to the admissibility of video surveillance evidence, the analysis will entail the following questions:

(i) Was it reasonable, in all the circumstances, to request surveillance?

(ii) Was the surveillance conducted in a reasonable manner?

(iii) Were other alternatives open to the company to obtain the evidence it sought?[71]

In some cases, the arbitrators have effectively incorporated question 3 into 1.[72] In general, video surveillance will never be "reasonable" unless the circumstances demonstrate that the employee's alleged injury/ disability may not be legitimate.[73] Further, cases for admissibility will be strengthened where the employer can demonstrate that they have taken less intrusive steps to confirm such suspicions before resorting to surveillance. For example, an employer should offer modified duties,[74] confront the employee of its suspicions, or demand further medical verification of the disability[75] before resorting to the use of video surveillance.

---

[71] See *Doman Forest Products Ltd. v. I.W.A., Local 1-357* (1990), 13 L.A.C. (4th) 275 (B.C. Arb. Bd.). Note that there has been a marked difference in arbitration decisions from provinces with privacy legislation in place from those which have not enacted a *Privacy Act*. For example, in *Doman* and *Steels Industrial Products*, *infra*, note 79, the arbitrators took "Charter values" into account when balancing the rights of the parties. That case took place in British Columbia where legislation governing privacy rights between private litigants is enacted. Conversely, in *Labatt Ontario Breweries (Toronto Brewery) v. Brewery, General & Professional Workers Union, Local 304* (1994), 42 L.A.C. (4th) 151 (Ont. Arb. Bd.) the arbitrator found that the absence of such privacy legislation in Ontario precluded the application of such "Charter values". Notwithstanding this distinction all the arbitration decisions appear to point to a consensus that the three part test (or a modified two step version) is to be applied.

[72] See *infra*, note 79; *Labatt*, *ibid.*

[73] See *New Flyer Industries Ltd. v. CAW-Canada, Local 3003* (2000), (sub nom. *New Flyer Industries Ltd. v. C.A.W.-Canada, Local 3003*) 85 L.A.C. (4th) 304 (Man. Arb. Bd.). See also *Toronto Transit Commission v. A.T.U., Local 113* (1999), 95 L.A.C. (4th) 402 (Ont. Arb. Bd.) in which the Arbitrator held that the employer's decision to continue conducting surveillance of the employee's home, after successfully contacting the employee in question, was unreasonable.

[74] See *Labatt*, *supra*, note 71.

[75] See *Air Canada v. C.U.P.E.*, [1995] C.L.A.D. No. 114 (Can. Arb. Bd.) where an employer hired a private investigator to undertake video surveillance of a flight attendant who suffered a lower back injury while at work. The arbitrator applied the three part test set out in *Doman*, *supra*, note 71, and refused to admit the

The three part admissibility test outlined above was first implemented in *Doman Forest Products Ltd. v. I.W.A., Local 1-357*,[76] a British Columbia decision that addressed the admissibility of video tape surveillance evidence. Video surveillance was conducted by an employer who had suspicions that the employee did not legitimately suffer from injury. The union challenged the videotape's admissibility at the arbitration. The arbitrator applied the three part test outlined above, and determined that the video surveillance was inadmissible.

The same test was applied in the Ontario case, *Labatt Ontario Breweries (Toronto Brewery) v. Brewery, General & Professional Workers Union, Local 304*.[77] The employer had conducted video surveillance of an employee because of repeated absenteeism from work. This particular time, the employee had been absent from work due to an alleged car accident. The video surveillance showed the employee engaged in strenuous physical activity of a kind which did not correspond to an individual who was to be physically incapacitated. The arbitrator found that the employee's absenteeism did not justify the surveillance, given that the company appeared to treat such absenteeism as non-culpable. The arbitrator took particular account of the fact that no offer of modified work was ever made to the employee despite the company having a modified work program in place.

The arbitrator in *Walbar Canada Inc. v. U.S.A., Local 9236*,[78] applied a modified version of the three part test (*i.e.* a two question test).[79] The employer felt that the employee's injured ankle should not have prevented his return to work and terminated his employment when he failed to attend three separate pre-arranged appointments to have his ankle examined by the company doctor. The employer then conducted video surveillance of the

---

videotape evidence. Significant was the fact that the employer had been suspicious for a long while and yet never had its medical director or other medical staff carry out examinations of the employee. It was held that it was not reasonable in all the circumstances for the employer to conduct video surveillance of the employee without first confronting the employee of its suspicions and further informing her that it intended to pursue the matter to ascertain the state of her health.

[76] *Supra*, note 71.
[77] *Labatt*, *supra*, note 71.
[78] Dated April 22, 1993, unreported.
[79] This two part test is from *Steels Industrial Products v. Teamsters Union, Local 213* (1991), 24 L.A.C. (4th) 259 (B.C. Arb. Bd.) where the arbitrator found that the third question in the *Doman* test could be considered part of the first. See also *Greater Vancouver Regional District v. G.V.R.D.E.U.* (1996), 57 L.A.C. (4th) 113 (B.C. Arb. Bd.) where the arbitrator, upon review of the case law, applied the two part formulation of the test for admissibility as set out in *Steels*.

employee so as to collect further evidence to use as additional grounds for his termination. The union held that this was an invasion of the employee's privacy.

Two points were determinative with respect to the first part of the test. First, the medical staff and the employee's own doctor diagnosed the injury as a minor one and that full recovery would take place within two to three weeks. Additionally, as the employee avoided all contact with the employer, this prevented the employer from communicating with the employee and being informed as to the extent of the injury. Second, the employer received information that the employee was working as a superintendent in an apartment building, notwithstanding his alleged total disability.

As for the second part of the test, the arbitrator found that the video surveillance was conducted in a reasonable manner since it was carried out on public property where the employee was open to public scrutiny. Consequently, the surveillance was not intrusive in the sense that it did not seek to trespass upon private places, such as the employee's apartment. Accordingly, the arbitrator held that it was reasonable for the employer to request the surveillance, and further, that the surveillance was conducted in a reasonable manner.

Another factor in evaluating the reasonableness of video surveillance is dishonesty. Examples of an employee's previous dishonesty will further justify an employer's choice to undertake video surveillance and may obviate the need for the steps described above. In particular, arbitrators have appreciated that it may not be realistic to confront an employee with suspicions where the employee has demonstrated dishonesty.[80]

For example, in *Canadian Pacific Ltd. v. Brotherhood of Maintenance of Way Employees*[81] an employee was terminated when video surveillance evidence undertaken by the employer showed that he was not suffering, as alleged, from a work-related back injury. The employer conducted the video surveillance for the following reasons: a supervisor observed the employee walking with no signs of discomfort four days after the alleged injury; a doctor who first examined the employee reported that he felt that the employee was "pulling a scam" and that there was nothing wrong with him; the employee had provided false information to the Workers' Compensation Board in a previous application for benefits; and the employee had a long record of absenteeism caused by on-the-job injuries. The union objected to the admissibility of the videotape stating that it was an invasion of privacy.

Upon review of the case law the arbitrator set out the test in terms of the following two-part analysis:

---

[80] *Canadian Pacific Ltd. v. B.M.W.E.* (1996), 59 L.A.C. (4th) 111 (Can. Arb. Bd.).
[81] *Ibid.*

1. Was it reasonable, in all of the circumstances, to undertake surveillance of the employee's off-duty activity?

2. Was the surveillance conducted in a reasonable way, which is not unduly intrusive and which corresponds fairly with acquiring information pertinent to the employer's legitimate interests?

Applying the test, the arbitrator held that conducting video surveillance was justifiable in this case. The arbitrator determined that the employer did not have any other reasonable alternatives open to it given the employee's prior willingness to deceive the Workers Compensation Board, and the medical opinion that the employee was pretending to be disabled. In fact, the arbitrator stated that it would have been "naively unrealistic, and indeed counterproductive to determining the truth, for the Company to have communicated its suspicions or concerns to the employee . . ., as it had little reason to expect a truthful answer".[82]

The actual type or nature of the supposed injury is another factor which plays into the reasonableness of surveillance. If the injury is difficult to verify medically, then a doctor's report may be deemed to be of limited usefulness. In these circumstances, surreptitious surveillance may be the only practical way to confirm suspicions.[83]

When the employer is an arm of government, the protection found in section 8 of the *Canadian Charter of Rights and Freedoms* will also be a consideration in determining if video surveillance is permissible. In *A.T.U., Local 569 v. Edmonton (City)*,[84] the Court of Queen's Bench concluded that the Charter was applicable and rejected the city's argument that the Charter was not engaged when the city was involved in private actions such as dealings with its employees. The Court reasoned, however, that it is not the nature of the act that exposes the city to Charter standards, it is the fact of the city's status as a form of government entity.

The Court continued its analysis and looked at the issue of whether or not the employees in this instance had a reasonable expectation of privacy. Relying heavily on Supreme Court jurisprudence, the Court said that if an individual has reasonable grounds to believe his communications are private

---

[82] The company had also offered the employee modified duties and the evidence was recorded in areas where the employee was visible to the public.

[83] See *Western Grocers v. U.F.C.W.U., Local 1400* (unreported) a Saskatchewan decision dated July 21, 1995 where it was held that is was reasonable to conduct the video surveillance since the nature of the injury was such that there were no objective tests to prove the extent of pain and there were few other alternatives open to the employer to obtain the evidence sought.

[84] 2004 ABQB 280, 2004 CarswellAlta 435 (Alta. Q.B.).

7.2.4 PRIVACY IN EMPLOYMENT

in the sense that his words will only be heard by the person he is addressing, the unauthorized surreptitious electronic recording of those communications will be perceived as an intrusion on a reasonable expectation of privacy. However, the Court also expressed its opinion that, since the Charter did not create a right to privacy itself (just a right to be free from an invasion of that privacy), any violation of the section 8 Charter protection could only occur if an individual reasonably feels, wants or believes that his or her actions are or ought to remain private.

Importantly, the Court then says:

> It is generally thought that when an individual is in a public place, his or her actions are not private at all, but fully public. In those circumstances, it cannot be said that the individual has a reasonable expectation of privacy. This is not an application of the risk analysis rejected in *Duarte*, but is an acknowledgement that the privacy that people can expect to enjoy in our society does not generally extend to their public activities.

Later, the Court acknowledged that some public action may still attract a reasonable expectation of privacy if the circumstances are right, but in this case, the surveillance undertaken by the city was of a public place and was of public activities engaged by an employee. The employee was in a place of business open to the public and there was no evidence that the employee took precautions from being observed. Therefore, he could not have a reasonable expectation of privacy.[85]

The introduction of private sector privacy legislation is now also making its way into the mix when deciding if the use of video surveillance to monitor employees outside the workforce is appropriate. In *Ross v. Rosedale Transport Ltd.*,[86] the arbitrator was faced with a claim by a laid-off employee that the employer's use of video surveillance was contrary to the *Personal Information Protection and Electronic Documents Act* and therefore could not be admitted as evidence in the grievance proceeding.

The employee had been fired because the employer believed the employee was not as injured as the employee had explained. Because of the employee's alleged injury, he had been re-assigned but the employer became suspicious that the employee's alleged back injury was not that serious

---

[85] Without explaining why, the Court then found that since the employee did not have a reasonable expectation of privacy (or any other right to privacy found in law), the video tape surveillance could be used against him in employment related matters. The Court seems to have ignored the remaining tests for admissibility of such evidence that exist notwithstanding whether or not the Charter is triggered.

[86] (2003), 2003 CarswellNat 3620, [2003] C.L.A.D. No. 237 (Can. Arb. Bd.).

when he found out that the employee was going to help family members move over the weekend. The employer surreptitiously obtained video footage of the employee over the course of the weekend and later terminated him as a result of the faked injury.

First in dealing with the jurisdictional and threshold questions raised, the arbitrator said:

> It is common ground between the parties that the Act applies to Rosedale as it is a federal work, undertaking or business and interprovincial in nature, as the trucking operations extend beyond the borders of the Province of Ontario. It was also my view and remains that the video surveillance as captured on tape contains personal information, namely, the physical movements of an identifiable individual in carrying furniture from his house to a truck parked in his driveway.

Then the arbitrator examined section 7(1)(b) of the Act, which stipulates that an organization may collect personal information without the knowledge or consent of the individual only if it is reasonable to expect that the collection with the knowledge or consent of the individual would compromise the availability or the accuracy of the information and the collection is reasonable for purposes related to investigating a breach of an agreement. The arbitrator quickly conceded that there was no doubt that had the employee known about the collection, that it would have compromised the accuracy of the information collected.

However, the arbitrator continued by examining the first part of the test in section 7(1)(b), *i.e.*, whether or not the video surveillance was reasonable for purposes related to investigating a breach of his employment agreement. In the arbitrator's view, the principles emanating from previous jurisprudence[87] on the issue of video surveillance played a key role in determining this part of the question:

> In my opinion, these general principles are also apposite in the interpretation of section 7(1) of the Act given the purpose of the Act as prescribed in section 3. In my view, the question that must be answered is whether or not it was reasonable for Rosedale to conduct the video surveillance without the knowl-

---

[87] The arbitrator quoted *Transit Windsor v. A.T.U., Local 616* (2001), 99 L.A.C. (4th) 295 (Ont. Arb. Bd.) for the proposition that the following three questions (referred to above) had to be looked at when performing the balancing act between the employee's right of privacy and the employer's right to protect its own interest: 1. Was it reasonable, in all the circumstances, to request a surveillance? 2. Was the surveillance conducted in a reasonable manner? 3. Were other alternatives open to the company to obtain the evidence it sought?

edge and consent of Ross for purposes related to the investigation of an alleged breach of the employment agreement.

In this case, there was absolutely no other reason or previous conduct that warranted suspicion. There were also a number of other means available to the employer to test the veracity of the employee's injury allegations. Quoting *Canadian Pacific Ltd. v. Brotherhood of Maintenance of Way Employees*, the arbitrator said:

> As a general rule, (the employer's interests) does not justify resort to random video surveillance in the form of an electronic web, cast like a net, to see what it might catch. Surveillance is an extraordinary step which can only be resorted to where there is, beforehand, reasonable and probable cause to justify it. What constitutes such cause is a matter to be determined on the facts of each case.

Having concluded that the use of video surveillance was not reasonable, the arbitrator found that the personal information had been collected in violation of the Act and excluded the evidence.

The analysis undertaken by the arbitrator in *Ross* seems consistent with the analysis adopted by the federal Assistant Privacy Commissioner when the issue of surreptitious videotaping was brought before her as a possible violation of the *Personal Information Protection and Electronic Documents Act*. In *PIPED Act Case Summary #269*, the Assistant Privacy Commissioner was asked to rule that an employer's hiring of a private investigator to capture video evidence of an employee performing tasks inconsistent with the employee's assertions of injury. However, in all the circumstances of that matter, the Assistant Commissioner found that the purposes of the collection of personal information by use of the video camera was reasonable in the circumstances. In coming to this conclusion, she found that the employer supplied ample evidence: to prove the organization's suspicion that the relationship of trust had been broken, that showed that it has exhausted all other means of obtaining the information that it required in less privacy-invasive ways, and that it limited the collection to the purposes to the greatest extent possible.

7.3 EMERGING SURVEILLANCE ISSUES

In addition to the use of video and e-mail surveillance in the workplace, new technologies are further expanding the ways in which employers can monitor employee conduct and performance at work. Modern networked systems can interrogate computers to determine which software is being run, how often, and in what manner. Audit trails provide employers with a profile of each employee and a complete view of how workers interact with their machines. Software programs allow employers to control individual computers and remotely modify or suspend programs on any machine. Employers can measure how much an employee is using their computer by the amount of time the computer is idle during the day and by calculating the number of keystrokes the employee enters into a word processing program within a specified time. Certain inexpensive programs enable employers to compile and analyze the above-mentioned information to develop performance profiles of their employees.[88]

A recent case in Alberta illustrates, however, that there are limits to employers' use of such technology.[89] The Parkland Regional Library installed keystroke logging software on the computer of an information technology employee, unbeknownst to the employee, due to the Director's concerns about the employee's work performance. When the employee discovered the software, he disabled the program and filed a complaint with Alberta's Privacy Commissioner. The Privacy Commissioner stated that despite the fact that no one other than the complainant himself read the information collected prior to the program being disabled, the material was personal information. Even if most or all of the information that was collected from the employee was work-related activity, all of it had a personal component in this case because it was used to determine how much work he did, or his style or manner of doing it, or his own choices and how to prioritize it. Additionally, the employee's banking information was collected by the software program.

The library relied on section 33(c) of the *Freedom of Information and Protection of Privacy Act*, R.S.A. 2000, c. F-25, which permits the collection of information relating directly to and necessary for an operating program or activity of a public body, to argue that the collection was necessary to manage the employee due to concerns about his productivity and his use of his time at work. However, on reviewing the evidence, the Privacy Commissioner expressed doubt that a perceived shortfall in the employee's productivity prompted the decision to install the keystroke logging software. Rather, the Director's testimony indicated that the software was installed following the employee's performance appraisal interview because she felt that he had not 'heard' her concerns that he was not a 'team player' and was too independent in his approach to problem-solving. Further, the Privacy Commissioner noted that during the interview, the Director had not raised any concern with the employee about his lack of productivity, use of his

---

[88] Marc Rotenberg & Cedric Laurant, "Privacy & Human Rights 2004: An International Survey of Privacy Laws and Developments", November 2004 at 58, 59.
[89] Alberta Office of Information and Privacy Commissioner, Order F2005-003, June 24, 2005.

working time or his way of prioritizing tasks. Therefore, it was unclear as to what concerns prompted the Director to direct the installation of the software.

The Privacy Commissioner held that the Parkland Library did not have the authority under section 33 of the Act to collect the complainant's personal information through keystroke logging, and stated that information collected by keystroke logging software becomes "necessary" within the meaning of section 33(c) of the Act only when there is no less intrusive way of collecting sufficient information to address a particular management issue. In this case, there were less-intrusive means available for the library to effectively manage its employees.

Other technologies, such as location badges and geostationary satellite-based mobile communications systems can track the geographic movements of mobile workers to ensure that they can be located at all times. Some telephone surveillance systems can record and analyze all phone transactions and determine patterns of use by grouping calls into networks. Employers can also monitor or access employees' voice mail systems via default pass codes.[90]

Biometrics is also providing employers with advanced methods of enhancing workplace security. In one case, bank employees complained to the Privacy Commissioner that their employer required them to consent to the collection of biometric information, specifically their voice print, so that the employees could access the bank's business applications, which were used to document work-related information and report employee absences. The employees considered this an invasion of privacy and also objected to the system prompting them to provide a reason for their absences (though they were unaware that providing reasons was not obligatory, since this was not evident to users of the applications).

The biometrics in question involved accessing a portal that used voice password technology to authenticate company employees by way of identifying the behavioural and physical characteristics of the way that an employee speaks. The bank provided the employees with documents that explained the technology, its purposes and uses, and assured them that their voice prints were secured in a tightly controlled database. Few individuals at the bank had the authority to view or remove a voice print record, and voice prints could not be altered or reverse engineered to synthesize a voice. Voice prints were to be deleted one month after an employee was no longer eligible to use the system and the technology company claimed that a voice print could only be used to identify an employee to log on to the system.

---

[90] *Ibid.* at 59.

The employer claimed that the applications using voice password technology were introduced for the purposes of security, efficiency, and cost-effectiveness. The Assistant Commissioner stated that job requirements which infringe on employees' privacy must be assessed in accordance with the reasonable person test under section 5(3) of *PIPEDA*, and held that while a voice print was an invasion of privacy on the person, she did not consider that the print disclosed much information about the employee in the circumstances of this case. In balancing the employees' privacy rights against the bank's needs, a reasonable person would likely view the bank's purposes to be appropriate. The purposes for the voice print system were reasonable and had been explained to the employees, and an alternative system was not likely to provide the same level of security. However, the Assistant Commissioner held that the system component which prompted employees to disclose medical reasons for work-related absences was excessive and requested that the company change the application to exclude the requirement for such information.[91]

"Blogging" (web logging, or online journal entries) has emerged as a new Internet trend and appears to be on the rise with employees and contractors both in and outside the workplace, causing conflict between workers and employers over the propriety of commentary about employers on the Internet. In the U.S., employees can be terminated even if blogging takes place from home on their own time if their employer comes across the employee's blog on the Internet and is offended by the content. Most U.S. states (45 at present) offer no protection against being fired in such instances. Only five states have enacted laws limiting an employer's right to dismiss an employee for off-duty activity that is not related to their job.[92]

Delta Air Lines, Friendster, Google, and Microsoft have all reportedly fired employees or contractors over the content of their blogs, which contained criticisms of their employer or colleagues or disclosed confidential company information. In particular, one employee with eights years experience at Delta Air Lines was suspended and subsequently fired for posting suggestive pictures of herself in uniform inside the company airplane on the Internet in connection with her blog. Even where employees create an anonymous blog that offends their employer, a company could attempt to identify the employee by filing a "John Doe" lawsuit and sending a subpoena

---

[91] Privacy Commissioner of Canada, September 3rd, 2004, Summary #281.
[92] CNET News.com, "Blogging on the job" by Declan McCullagh and Alorie Gilbert, March 8, 2005, online: <http://news.com.com/2100-1030_3-5597010.html>; CNN.com, "Blog-linked firings prompt calls for better policies", March 6, 2005, online: <http://www.CNN.com/2005/TECH/internet/03/06/Firedforblogging.ap/index.html>.

to the blog hosting company. The increase in terminations of employees in relation to blogging suggests that although many companies have implemented policies prohibiting employee misuse of the Internet, few of the policies directly address blogging, particularly outside of the workplace.[93]

These emerging issues clearly signal that an employee's privacy rights are not absolute and must be considered in light of the employer's right to control workplace activity and preserve its business reputation through privacy-invasive technologies and employee monitoring.

---

[93] *Ibid.*

8

Medical and Genetic Information

8.1 MEDICAL INFORMATION

8.1.1 Introduction

Personal medical records are afforded substantial privacy protection via federal and provincial privacy and health legislation, constitutional law, human rights codes, and the common law. (For further information, see section 8.2.2 – *Legislation* under *Genetic Information & Privacy*). These protections are designed to safeguard individuals from the collection, use and disclosure of medical information without their consent, however, in the context of the workplace, case law has recognized a need to balance competing interests between an employee's privacy rights with an employer's obligation to operate their business in a safe and efficient manner.

8.1.2 Mandatory Medical Examinations

Federal and provincial occupational health and safety statutes and the common law place a duty on employers to take reasonable care and ensure that reasonable care is taken for the health, safety and welfare of all employees, as well as the public. This includes a duty to maintain a safe workplace, monitor employees' health and safety at work, and to maintain health and safety records. Likewise, the employee has a duty to ensure that he or she does not create risks to his or her own health or safety and that of others in or near the workplace.[1] Employers are also required to implement workplace surveillance programs to monitor the health and safety of employees. The Ontario *Occupational Health and Safety Act*,[2] for example, requires an employer to establish a medical surveillance program for the benefit of employees as prescribed; provide for safety-related medical examinations and tests for workers as prescribed; and where so prescribed, only permit a worker to work or be in a workplace who has undergone such

---

[1] *Canada Labour Code*, R.S.C. 1985, c. L-2, ss.125, 125(1), 126(1).
[2] *Occupation Health and Safety Act*, R.S.O. 1990, c. O.1.

medical examinations, tests or x-rays as prescribed and who is found to be physically fit to do the work in the workplace.[3]

Human rights legislation protects against discrimination in employment on the basis of disability or perceived disability, unless the employer can prove that the employee's disability prevents them from fulfilling a *bona fide* occupational requirement of the position, such as the ability to conduct work safely so as not to risk the health and safety of themselves and other employees, provided the employer has exhausted its efforts to accommodate the employee to the point of undue hardship. Human rights legislation and policies may limit the employer's scope regarding workplace safety measures by restricting the type of questions that an employer can ask of prospective and current employees regarding a disability or perceived disability. Specifically, section 7 of the *Canadian Human Rights Act*[4] states:

> It is a discriminatory practice, directly or indirectly, to refuse to employ or continue to employ any individual, or in the course of employment, to differentiate in relation to an employee, on a prohibited ground of discrimination.

The Supreme Court of Canada's decision in *Ontario Human Rights Commission v. Etobicoke (Borough)*[5] is authority for the proposition that a requirement imposed by an employer in the interest of safety must, in order to qualify as a *bona fide* occupational requirement, be reasonably necessary in order to eliminate a sufficient risk of damage. In ruling that the employer had not shown that compulsory retirement for two firefighters over the age of 60 was a *bona fide* occupational qualification and requirement for the employment concerned, the Court emphasized:

> A *bona fide* occupational qualification must be imposed honestly, in good faith, and in the sincerely held belief that it is imposed in the interests of adequate performance of the work involved with reasonable dispatch, safety and economy and not for ulterior or extraneous reasons that could defeat the Code's purpose. The qualification must be objectively related to the employment concerned, ensuring its efficient economical performance without endangering the employee or others.

Under numerous occupational health and safety statutes, an employee's consent is required before an employer can include him or her in a prescribed medical surveillance program, however, certain statutes oblige employees to undergo medical examinations required by the Act and reg-

---

[3] *Ibid.*, ss. 26, 27, 28.
[4] *Canadian Human Rights Act*, R.S.C 1985, c. H-6, s. 7 [*CHRA*].
[5] [1982] 1 S.C.R. 202 (S.C.C.).

ulations. In *School District No. 39 (Vancouver) v. B.C.T.F.*,[6] the British Columbia Court of Appeal upheld an arbitrator's argument that requiring employees to undergo a medical examination on the advice of a medical officer did not violate section 7 (right to "life, liberty, and security" of the person) of the Charter. The teacher had been behaving irrationally and inappropriately towards colleagues and the school administrator and had received numerous disciplinary letters.

Concern for the health and safety of students and employees prompted the school board to order the teacher to undergo a psychiatric examination under the authority of the *School Act*, R.S.B.C. 1996, c. 412. The teacher repeatedly refused to undergo the examination and was subsequently required to take forced sick leave. The teacher's union argued that her Charter right to life, liberty and security had been violated, however, the Court ruled that sections 7 and 8 (right to be free from "unreasonable search or seizure") of the Charter did not encompass protection against intrusions affecting only economic or employment rights. The right to liberty did not include the right to choose not to undergo medical exams under the Act and continue in employment in defiance of it.

In the absence of specific authority under statute or collective agreements, an employer does not have inherent power to submit an individual to a medical examination. However, case law suggests that employers may be permitted to refuse to put an employee back to work without adequate information about the employee's fitness to perform their duties. In *Re Shell Canada Products Ltd. v. Canadian Association of Industrial, Mechanical & Allied Workers, Local 112*,[7] the arbitrator did not allow the employer to demand that an employee, who had pulled a muscle in his arm, undergo a physical examination by a company doctor or compel the employee to divulge confidential information regarding his medical condition. Nor could the employee be punished for insubordination for refusing to consent to a medical exam. However, the arbitrator ruled that where an employer has reasonable cause to believe that the employee is unsafe or unfit to work, the employer may refuse to permit the employee to return to work or dismiss the employee by virtue of incapacity to perform the work.

The decision in *Re NAV Canada v. C.A.T.C.A.*[8] established that although an employer is not entitled to sensitive medical information about an employee, an employer may request an employee to consent to the release of medical information to a physician retained by the employer and to

---

[6] (2003), 224 D.L.R. (4th) 63 (B.C. C.A.), leave to appeal refused (2003), 109 C.R.R. (2d) 188 (note) (S.C.C.).
[7] (1990), 14 L.A.C. (4th) 75 (B.C. Arb. Bd.).
[8] (1998), 74 L.A.C. (4th) 163 (Can. Arb. Bd.).

undergo a medical examination by that physician where the position involves risks to public safety. The Arbitrator concluded that if, in the all circumstances, the request is reasonable and the employer can only be reasonably satisfied by the disclosure of evidence to its own medical advisors or by its own physician or one agreed to between the parties, "the employee may have to choose between suffering the continued administrative consequences, or consenting to the release [of medical information] or the examination".

This dispute involved a grievance filed by the Canadian Air Traffic Controllers' Association against NAV Canada over whether NAV Canada had the authority to require an employee to consent to the release of his or her medical information to the employer's physician and whether the employer could require an employee to submit to a medical examination by that physician, failing which, sanctions such as discipline, withholding sick leave benefits, or refusal to allow the employee to work could be imposed. The arbitrator ruled that the employer is not entitled to sensitive medical information and has no independent right to require disclosure of medical information or third party medical examination which can be enforced by disciplinary action. However, an employer is entitled to know whether an employee is fit or not, and any limitations which may have to be accommodated. In this case, the collective agreement was broad enough to justify administrative action to withhold sick leave benefits or refuse to allow an employee to return or continue to work.

Employees and applicants may refuse to undergo medical examinations, or alternatively, provide misleading or incomplete medical information for fear that positive results will invite social stigma and prove detrimental to their current employment status or to future career opportunities. Employers, on the other hand, are required by law to provide a safe and healthy work environment. Occupational health and safety statutes, human rights legislation and other laws attempt to balance these competing interests by imposing duties on both employers and employees to ensure a safe workplace, while preventing employers from obtaining information about employees' health or disabilities that is not strongly related to the duties required of the position.

8.1.3 Medical Certificates

Legislation and case law have established that the employer has a right and an obligation to ensure an employee's fitness to perform the tasks required of their position in a manner that ensure the health and safety of others in the workplace. However, an employer must have reasonable and probable grounds for questioning an employee's capacity to do the work before demanding medical certification of fitness or better certification than that provided by the employee.

In *Masterfeeds and U.F.C.W., Local 1518*,[9] the arbitrator determined that the employer had reasonable grounds to question the employee's assertion that he was fit to return to work following a medical leave of absence due to substance abuse, since the information provided by the employee's physician indicated that he continued to have difficulty with substance abuse. The employee, who occupied a safety-sensitive position as a tractor-trailer driver, agreed to submit to an independent medical examination but revoked his authorization to release the report to his employer after learning that the results indicated that he was not fit to resume his duties. The employer subsequently dismissed the employee, asserting that the revocation gave rise to just cause.

The arbitrator ruled that where an employee seeks to return to work after illness or injury, an employer can refuse to permit the employee from resuming his or her duties where the employer is not satisfied that the employee can capably fulfill their work duties. However, an employer does not have the right to discipline an employee for failing to provide additional information, or for refusing to be examined by a doctor chosen by the employer. The employee was reinstated, though his return to active duty was conditional on providing proper medical certification.

At issue in *Ontario Nurses' Association v. St. Joseph's Hospital*[10] was the type of information that an employer can require in a medical certificate. In this case, the arbitrator ruled that in fulfilling its duty to assure that employees are fit to return to work without compromising the safety of themselves and others, an employer does not require a specific diagnosis of the employee's condition provided that the medical certificate supports a safe return to work. In this case, a nurse who had been on sick leave informed the hospital that she needed time off for surgery. The hospital requested that she complete its short-term disability form, authorizing her physician to release specific medical information, including a diagnosis of her present condition.

The nurse refused to complete the form due to concern about the hospital's ability to keep the information confidential. In his decision, the arbitrator stated that the hospital was required to show some flexibility in ensuring an employee's safe return to work, and must restrict the types of questions on the medical certificate to those of a more general nature, such as confirmations that the employee was physically and mentally capable of returning to work, that her judgment was not impaired for any reason, and

---

[9] (2000), 92 L.A.C. (4th) 341 (B.C. Arb. Bd.).
[10] [2002] O.L.A.A. No. 869.

that she had been totally incapacitated from performing her duties during her absence.

An arbitrator ruled similarly in *B.C. Teacher's Federation v. B.C. Public School Employers' Association*,[11] regarding how much information an employer can require in a certificate for extended and partial medical leave. Here, the arbitrator determined that a school board could unilaterally introduce a policy requiring that teachers submit detailed medical certificates with applications for medical leave where the policy was reasonable and the collective agreement was silent on the matter. However, the employer was not entitled to request a specific diagnosis of an employee's health problem, inquire as to when the employee first saw the physician, or elicit information regarding the teacher's ability to perform partial duties where the teacher had requested an extended medical leave.

In a case involving a private sector employer, an employee of a telecommunications company who was on extended sick leave complained to the Privacy Commissioner of Canada that his employer was collecting more medical information than was necessary, and was disclosing it to company managers without his consent.[12] The company's policy required employees on extended sick leave to sign a consent form authorizing his or her physician to release medical information regarding the employee's medical condition, treatment, and prognosis to the company's occupational health professionals.

The Commissioner determined that the company's occupational health staff, doctors, and nurses were bound by their respective codes of ethics to provide managers only with information pertaining to the abilities and limitations of the employee, and that the company had policies and procedures in place to safeguard employee medical information. The Commissioner could find no evidence supporting the employee's claims that health care employees had disclosed his medical information to managers without his consent. Therefore, the Commissioner found that the company's purposes for collecting the employee's medical information was legitimate and it had met all of its obligations under the *PIPEDA*.

When a situation necessitates an employee to take emergency sick leave from work, the employer may subsequently require the employee to produce evidence that is reasonable in the circumstance to confirm that the employee is entitled to the leave, pursuant to section 50(7) of the *Employment Standards Act, 2000*, S.O. 2000, c. 41. In *Tillbury Assembly Ltd and United Auto Workers, Local 251*,[13] an employee was given a one-day sus-

---

[11] [2002] L.C.C. No. 4454.
[12] Privacy Commissioner of Canada, February 17, 2003, Summary #118.
[13] (2004), 124 L.A.C. (4th) 375 (Ont. Arb. Bd.).

pension for failing to follow company policy requiring that she produce a doctor's note after leaving her shift early with a severe headache causing blurry vision and one of her eyes to swell almost fully closed. The employee had experienced similar headaches prior to this incident and had an absenteeism problem, thus, she had been told on previous occasions that the company required a doctor's note for medical absences.

The arbitrator concluded that as the employee's supervisors did not testify that they did not believe that she was suffering form a severe headache in this instance, the supervisors merely applied the company policy requiring the doctor's note without considering the situation. The arbitrator ruled that requiring the employee to obtain a doctor's note was not reasonable in the circumstances and expunged the suspension from her record.

8.1.4 Medical Records

Case law emphasizes that although an individual does not own his or her medical records, the individual has an inherent right to access their own medical information, subject to such access being in their best interests. The Supreme Court of Canada decision in *McInerney v. MacDonald*[14] affirmed:

> Information about oneself revealed to a doctor acting in a professional capacity remains, in a fundamental sense, one's own. . . . The confiding of the information to the physician for medical purposes gives rise to an expectation that the patient's interest in and control of the information will continue. . . . Disclosure serves to reinforce the patient's faith in her treatment and to enhance the trust inherent in the doctor-patient relationship. As well, the duty of confidentiality that arises from the doctor-patient relationship is meant to encourage disclosure of information and communication between doctor and patient.

The case of *Ontario Human Rights Commission v. Dofasco Inc.*[15] defines an employer's right to access an employee's medical records when the employee makes a complaint of discrimination against the employer on the basis of handicap. The Dofasco employee went on disability leave for four years following a number of injuries sustained in her job as a crane operator. In the fourth year of her leave, the employer offered her a position as a switchboard operator. The employee requested time to speak with the specialist who was treating her, however, her employer demanded that she attend at Dofasco Medical Services and report to work two weeks later. The employee attended Dofasco Medical services as ordered, but did not report

---

[14] [1992] S.C.R. 138 (S.C.C.).
[15] (2001), [2001] L.C.C. No. 406, 208 D.L.R. (4th) 276 (Ont. C.A.).

to work on the date set by her employer. Dofasco then terminated her, alleging just cause.

The employee filed a complaint with the Ontario Human Rights Commission, claiming that Dofasco had discriminated against her because of physical handicap, and the Commission referred her complaint to a Board of Inquiry. Dofasco submitted before the Board that the employee had failed to submit any documentation that she could perform even light duties, and brought a motion requesting that a number of documents be produced, including the employee's medical records, a list of all medical practitioners who had examined or treated her, and the details of those visits. The Board granted the motion in part, requiring the employee to provide Dofasco with a list of the medical practitioners who had treated her during her four-year medical leave, the doctor's areas of expertise, the dates of the visits, and the conditions for which she was treated.

The Human Rights Commission brought an application before the Ontario Divisional Court for judicial review of the Board's decision, arguing that the Board had exercised its discretion unreasonably in requiring the employee to disclose privileged medical information that was not related to her condition. The Divisional Court dismissed the Commission's application and the Commission appealed the decision to the Ontario Court of Appeal. The Court of Appeal allowed the appeal in part. Weighing the need to protect privileged or irrelevant information against Dofasco's right to full disclosure, the Court of Appeal ruled that the employee's right to privacy would be irreparably violated if all of the information requested were fully disclosed. Where a complainant's right to privacy would be jeopardized by such disclosure, the complainant's privacy interests will prevail.

Case law is clear that an employer cannot refuse an employee's written request to access to their medical files or release their file to an authorized agency. In *Ontario Nurses' Association v. North York General Hospital*,[16] a nurse was seeking to return to work after an extended medical leave due to an injury at work, however, the employer would not allow her to return. On consulting her union, the union instructed her to authorize the employer's Occupational Health Department to release a copy of her health file to the union, in accordance with the employer's "Confidentiality of Employee Information" policy which allowed for such release to authorized agencies on written consent of the employee.

In anticipation that the union might file a grievance against the hospital, the hospital directed the Occupation Health Department not to release the health file to the union unless the employee also consented to provide a copy to the hospital's Human Resources Department. Though her employer

---

[16] (2004), [2004] O.L.A.A. No. 109, 2004 CarswellOnt 1723 (Ont. Arb. Bd.).

did not preclude the employee from viewing her health file in the presence of an employee in the Occupation Health Department, the employer would not allow her to make copies of her file. The union then filed grievances on behalf of the employee, alleging that the employer's actions were improper and seeking a declaration that the employer had violated the collective agreement and certain statutes. The union also filed a grievance protesting the employer's refusal to return the employee to work, which was settled, leaving the former to be resolved.

The arbitrator ruled that the employer, by imposing the condition that the nurse consent to providing management with a copy of her health file as well, had breached the article of the collective agreement that prohibited the employer from discrimination or interference with respect to any nurse by reason of her exercising her rights under the collective agreement. The union was the employee's representative and in that capacity could be privy to information about the employee which the employer could not expect to access simply because the union did. Additionally, the employer's access to the employee's health file was unwarranted, since the union was merely conducting an investigation as opposed to filing a grievance when it requested the files.

An employee may be required to disclose their medical records at an arbitration hearing, pursuant to labour relations statutes and case law. In determining the appropriateness of such a disclosure, the arbitrator in *West Park Hospital and ONA*[17] established a five-step test relating to relevance to the issues in dispute and some analysis of prejudice. In this case, a nurse had been discharged for incompetence and the employer's request for pre-hearing disclosure of her medical records was denied. The five elements required to determine relevance and prejudice are:

1. Information requested must be arguably relevant

2. The information must be particularized so that there is no dispute as to what is being requested

3. The board should be satisfied that the information is not being requested as a fishing expedition

4. There must be a nexus between the information requested and the positions in dispute at the hearing

5. The board should be satisfied that disclosure will not cause undue prejudice to the employee

---

[17] (1993), 37 L.A.C. (4th) 160 (Ont. Arb. Bd.).

8.1.5 PRIVACY IN EMPLOYMENT

The arbitrator in *Re Becker Milk Co. and Milk & Bread Drivers, Dairy Employees, Caterers & Allied Employees, Local 647*[18] adopted this five-step test to ensure a fair hearing, in determining whether the employee's union should be ordered to produce all information relevant to the employee's medical condition before the employer is require to proceed with its case. The employee was dismissed after writing numerous threatening letters to the company's vice-president for which he was charged under the *Criminal Code*. The employee was subsequently diagnosed with bipolar disorder and it was determined that at the time of his dismissal, he was in fact suffering from delusions and psychotic breaks. The arbitrator stated that some medical information such as that relating to mental disorders tend to stigmatize individuals, and in such cases, a higher onus must be put on the requesting party to satisfy the arbitrator as to why this information is essential. However, the arbitrator ruled given the nature of the employee's letters, the doctor's reports, and the company's concerns over the employee's conduct, the pre-hearing production of pertinent medical records and a medical examination of the employee by a doctor of the employer's choice was necessary to ensure a fair hearing.

8.1.5 Monitoring & Surveillance/Surveillance as Evidence

(See Chapter 7 - Video Surveillance outside the Workplace)

8.2 GENETIC INFORMATION & PRIVACY

8.2.1 Introduction

Genetic information includes DNA sequence information revealed by a genetic test, and inferences that can be made from knowledge of the sequence. Genetic information may also be revealed by studying entire chromosomes, RNA, proteins, substances in blood or tissues, and medical imaging techniques; diagnosing a genetic disorder by clinical examination; or studying a person's family medical history. While rare, inherited monogenic diseases, such as Huntington's disease, involve a mutation in a single gene and can indicate a certainty of acquiring the disease. However, most genetic diseases, such as heart disease, cancer and Alzheimer's, involve many genes and often also involve environmental components, making it highly difficult to predict with certainty through genetic testing.[19]

---

[18] (1996), 53 L.A.C. (4th) 420 (Ont. Arb. Bd.).
[19] Canadian Biotechnology Advisory Committee, *Protecting Privacy in the Age of Genetic Information*, "Genetics, Privacy and Discrimination" by Eugene Osca-

MEDICAL AND GENETIC INFORMATION   8.2.1

The information generated by DNA testing can be very precise in indicating that a particular mutation is or is not present, though such precision is not especially helpful in predicting future health conditions. Thus, genetic information tends to contemplate possibilities rather than certainties, since most genetic tests reveal risk factors without necessarily addressing an individual's current physical or mental health status.[20] The use of such potentially imprecise information has disquieting implications in employment, as the information could be incorporated into decision-making by employers and insurance companies, allowing them to draw conclusions about the health status of employees and adversely affect the employability, insurability and career prospects of individuals.

DNA can uniquely identify an individual and their physical and behavioural characteristics. The amount of information that can be extracted and inferred from a single DNA sample is potentially staggering, and if stored in genetic data banks or "biobanks", the sample has the potential to reveal information about an individual far into the future and beyond the purposes for which the individual first provided the sample.[21] "As more and more genetic links are uncovered, the holder of one blood sample may have access to a tremendous reservoir of deeply private, deeply personal, information about an individual."[22]

In fact, research into the development of DNA chip and micro-array technology is already in progress and soon will likely allow for the scanning of entire genes to detect a variety of mutations. Genetic tools will become faster, more efficient, and cheaper.[23] Therefore, the volume of information that can be extracted from one sample, the rapid speed of testing, and the link between genetics and computer technology underscore the need to assess the effectiveness of current regulatory schemes in Canada *vis-à-vis* their ability to protect individual privacy.

---

pella, (Ottawa: 2004 – Canadian Biotechnology Advisory Committee) at 8, 9 [*Oscapella*].

[20] Australian Health Ethics Committee, *Protection of Human Genetic Information*, Issues Paper 26, October 2001 at 86, 87 [*AHEC*].

[21] Canadian Biotechnology Advisory Committee, *Protecting Privacy in the Age of Genetic Information*, "Of Volume, Depth and Speed: The Challenges of Genetic Information" by Trudo Lemmens and Lisa Austin, (Ottawa: 2004 – publisher?) at 27, 28 [*Lemmens*].

[22] Mark Sabourin, *OHS Canada Magazine*, "Bad Blood", March, 1999, online: <www.ohscanada.com/virtual-issue/artucle/badblood.html>.

[23] *Ibid.*, at 1.

8.2.2 PRIVACY IN EMPLOYMENT

8.2.2 Legislation

At present, Canada has not enacted any legislation relating specifically to genetic information and privacy, apart from criminal legislation regarding the use of DNA in criminal investigations. Nor is there any specific prohibition against genetic testing in employment. Most of the laws which affect genetic privacy are more general in their application, and do not identify genetic privacy as requiring explicit legal protection.[24] However, these laws do provide a basic legal framework for dealing with genetic information and privacy. Such legislation includes constitutional law (i.e., the *Canadian Charter of Rights and Freedoms*), quasi-constitutional law (i.e., Quebec's *Charter of Human Rights and Freedoms*), federal and provincial human rights codes, federal and provincial data protection/privacy statutes, provincial health information protection legislation, laws governing professional confidentiality, statutory privacy torts in some provinces the emerging common law tort of invasion of privacy, and the criminal law (i.e., protections against physical intrusion).

In 1992, the Privacy Commissioner of Canada issued a report entitled *Genetic Testing and Privacy*, which made 22 recommendations regarding the need to protect the privacy and confidentiality of personal genetic information.[25] Since then, many technological advances have occurred that could have significant implications with respect to genetic privacy. Notably, the Privacy Commissioner's *Annual Report* (1999-2000) stated:

> In 1992, we recommended the government adopt legislation to ensure that genetic material was collected within a legal framework, that no one was forced to give up genetic material, that genetic testing would not be a condition of employment, and that no one would suffer discrimination for refusing to be tested. We also proposed amending the definition of personal information in the *Privacy Act* to ensure that it included both genetic samples and the information derived from their analysis.
>
> *Virtually all the recommendations have fallen on deaf ears.* With the costs of genetic tests falling, a lengthening list of conditions that tests can identify, and pressure building to develop comprehensive linked health information banks on Canadians, we still have no legal framework for this intrusive technology. We do not even know how and how much employers are using genetic testing.[26]

---

[24] Policy Research Initiative, *Genomics, Health and Society: Emerging Issues for Public Policy* edited by Bartha Maria Knoppers and Charles Schriver, (Ottawa: 2003) at 160.

[25] *Supra*, note 2 at 1, 18.

[26] *Supra*, note 10 at 159.

As indicated by the Privacy Commissioner, there is concern and reservation over the extent to which these laws are designed to protect against privacy threats posed by new biotechnologies and computer technologies. Consequently, the Commissioner along with many other experts in the field of genetic information and privacy are calling for significant reforms and amendments to current Canadian law to address and anticipate threats to genetic privacy in the future. Moreover, despite having a basic legal framework in place in Canada, it is clear that all of the present laws include exceptions to an individual's right to privacy, emphasizing that no privacy rights are absolute. In each circumstance, the competing interests of an individual employee must be weighed against societal interests and values, such as public health and safety.[27]

8.2.3 Screening, Monitoring and Discrimination: Implications on Hiring, Job Retention and Promotion

In the employment context, genetic information can be used by employers to assess suitability for employment, job performance and promotion, and the genetic consequences of exposure to hazardous workplace materials or environmental contaminants. As of 1990, there were no reports of systematic collection or use of genetic information in the employment setting in Canada, though it is possible that such information may already be part of employees' health files.[28]

It is unclear at present how human rights legislation and case law would extend to protect a pre-symptomatic employee with the likelihood of developing a disabling disease, or an asymptomatic employee with a genetic predisposition with the potential to acquire a future disability.[29] However, the decision in *Quebec (Commission des droits de la personne et des droits de la jeunesse) v. Montreal (City)*; *Quebec (Commission des droits de la personne et des droits de la jeunesse) v. Boisbriand (City)*[30] may provide useful insight.

In this case, the Supreme Court of Canada confirmed that the term "disability" extends to include perceived disability, even though human rights codes and Canada's *Charter of Rights and Freedoms* do not specifically enumerate perceived disability as a prohibited ground. The City of

---

[27] *Lemmens, supra,* note 8 at 22; Health Canada, "Selected Legal Issues in Genetic Testing: Guidance from Human Rights" by Derek Jones (Ottawa: Minister of Public Works and Government services, 2001) at 22 [*Jones*].
[28] *Ibid.* at 10, 21.
[29] *Oscapella, supra,* note 2 at 23; *AHEC, supra,* note 3 at 275.
[30] [2000] 1 S.C.R. 665 (S.C.C.).

8.2.3 PRIVACY IN EMPLOYMENT

Montreal had refused to hire one individual as a horticulturalist because the pre-employment medical exam revealed an anomaly of the spinal column. The City of Boisbriand dismissed another individual from his position as a police officer because he had Crohn's disease. The medical evidence in each case indicated that the individuals could perform the duties of the position and that they had no functional limitations, thus they filed complaints with the Commission alleging discrimination on the basis of handicap.

The Tribunal held that the individuals had no remedy under the Quebec *Charter of Human Rights and Freedoms* because they did not meet the definition of handicap, as their conditions did not result in functional limitations. The Quebec Court of Appeal reversed the Tribunal's decision and the cities of Montreal and Boisbriand appealed the ruling. The Supreme Court of Canada affirmed the Court of Appeal's ruling, concluding that a handicap may be real or perceived, and may exist without proof of physical limitations or other ailments other than those created by prejudice and stereotypes. The emphasis must be on the distinction, exclusion, or preference rather than the precise cause or origin of the biomedical condition.

This case illustrates that the law in Canada has broadly interpreted the notion of "handicap", suggesting that a pre-symptomatic or asymptomatic employee with a genetic trait that does not result in a present disability would likely be protected against discrimination based on a predisposition or a perceived predisposition to develop a disability in the future. Pursuant to human rights law, occupational health and safety legislation and case law, there is little evidence that medical testing, which includes genetic testing, can be justified unless an employer can show that such testing is required to fulfill its duty to ensure or enhance workplace safety and take reasonable care for the health and safety of its workers and the public. The extent to which an employer owes a duty of care to employees with genetic susceptibilities to workplace injuries or hazardous substances has yet to be considered.

It is plausible that in the near future, genetic testing providers, like drug testing providers, may attempt to persuade employers that testing is necessary to ensure a safe and productive workplace, despite the current uncertainty and unreliability of most genetic tests. As technology advances, however, employers may eventually be able to use inexpensive, commercially available genetic tests similar to home pregnancy test kits to expedite the testing process or perhaps surreptitiously test their employees through saliva or hair roots for genetic conditions or susceptibilities, thereby enabling possible discrimination against employees without their knowledge.[31]

---

[31] *Oscapella, supra*, note 2 at 22, 27.

The availability of these private test kits may make it far more feasible and less costly for an employer to test employees for genetic predispositions or conditions than to remove workplace hazards.

Case law provides a basis from which the courts might formulate a ruling in cases involving surreptitious testing by an employer. Though the seminal case *R. v. Dyment*[32] pertained to a criminal matter and involved the unreasonable search and seizure by the police of an unconscious patient's blood sample, the decision signals a particular distaste by the courts of surreptitious testing by an institution to advance its purposes, seriously violating the personal autonomy of the individual. The ruling established the following:

> The use of a person's body without his consent to obtain information about him invades an area of privacy essential to the maintenance of his human dignity. ... A violation of a person's body is much more serious than a violation of his office or even his home. The sense of privacy transcends the physical. The dignity of the human being is equally seriously violated when the use is made of bodily substances taken by others for medical purposes in a manner that does not respect that limitation.

This case, along with the decisions mentioned in section *8.1 – Medical Information*, emphasize the requirement of an individual's consent to undergo medical and genetic testing in employment, unless otherwise required by statute, contractual obligation or court order.

If the burden of health care costs shifts to the private sector in Canada as it has in the United States, Canadian employers will develop a much greater interest in acquiring genetic information about job applicants and current employees to ensure that their organization screens for "genetically superior" employees and carefully monitors their health during the course of their employment.[33] In other words, employers would have a larger stake in screening against and monitoring employees who may put themselves and others at risk in the workplace, have an increased susceptibility to occupational disease, or are likely to be absent from work for long periods

---

[32] [1988] 2 S.C.R. 417 (S.C.C.).

[33] The prevalence of genetic testing by U.S. employers prompted former President Bill Clinton to sign an Executive Order in February 2000 which prohibits federal departments and agencies from using genetic information in hiring or employment actions. By the end of 2000, 23 American States had also enacted legislation regarding the use of genetic information in employment, indicating a clear trend by federal and state governments to provide more comprehensive protection against discrimination in employment on the basis of genetic information or status.

of time as a result of their genetic conditions, so that the employer can minimize economic loss and increase productivity. Further, employees with the most promising genetic traits may be privy to better job opportunities or promotions, leaving asymptomatic or pre-symptomatic "genetic undesirables" to settle for less attractive positions or no employment opportunities at all.[34]

Workers compensation schemes, which have generally replaced common law claims by compensating sick or injured employees on a no-fault basis, are usually funded by compulsory insurance or self-insurance. Since employers cannot contract out of workers compensation, an employer could be motivated to seek to access an employee's or applicant's genetic information and screen out individuals who are more genetically predisposed to injuries or diseases caused by workplace conditions, as a means of minimizing employer premiums. Alternatively, employers could attempt to obtain waivers from employees who exhibit predispositions to avoid liability altogether for workplace injury or illness. Given the power imbalance inherent in employment relationships, there may be an element of coercion in workplace testing. Individuals may feel pressured to undergo testing or sign waivers as a condition of obtaining or maintaining employment and protecting career prospects.[35]

Conversely, an employer is entitled to the information, which could include medical and genetic test results, that is reasonably necessary to maintain a safe and healthy workplace and to operate a business, particularly where the employer has substantially invested in senior employees and employee training.[36] Further, an employer could argue that genetic testing, surveillance, and monitoring may be their best defense against liability resulting from an individual's false, inaccurate or incomplete disclosure of medical information.

---

[34] *Ibid.*, at 287, 291, 300.
[35] *AHEC, supra,* note 3, at 284, 285, 299; Ontario Workplace Safety Insurance Board, "Injured at Work? We're Here to Help", online: <http://www.wsib.on.ca/wsib/wsibsite.nsf/LookupFiles/DownloadableFileWSISGuide/$File/3576AWSIS.pdf>.
[36] See generally, CCH Canadian Limited, *Canada Labour Law Reports,* (2001) para. 6426; Béatrice Godard *et al., European Journal of Human Genetics,* "Genetic Information and Testing in Insurance and Employment: Technical, Social, and Ethical Issues", 2003, 11, Suppl 2 at S127 [*Godard*].

8.2.4 Impact on Eligibility for Health Benefits, Long Term Disability Insurance, Life Insurance

Insurance companies, especially life insurers, have collected and used medical information, including family medical histories for over a century.[37] An individual seeking to be insured has a legal obligation to disclose all information that is deemed relevant for calculating premiums and underwriting the insurance policy, such as age, gender, occupation, health status, lifestyle, tobacco and alcohol use, and family history.[38] While federal and provincial human rights legislation prohibits discrimination in employment, it exempts some areas like pensions and insurance plans from its ambit.[39] This implies that insurers could lawfully exclude an employee from insurance coverage or charge higher premiums on the basis of genetic status, with no legal recourse available to the applicant, thereby creating a genetic underclass.[40] On the other hand, healthy applicants might wish to undergo genetic testing and voluntarily disclose their test results in order to take advantage of cheaper premiums. Further, employees who know that they are at high risk for disease or injury for instance,[41] could exploit insurance companies by shopping around for companies with the best benefits or by purchasing substantial amounts of life insurance.

The argument in support of genetic testing arises in particular as a result of attempts by prospective policy holders to conceal unfavourable information or incorrectly disclose information in the underwriting process (an act termed as "adverse selection"), thereby allowing higher risk policyholders to pay lower premiums or apply for extended coverage while the insurer pays out more claims and the general cost of insurance increases. In turn, higher insurance premiums for the entire pool of insurance might provide a disincentive for low risk applicants to obtain insurance.[42] Further, since family history is already used as a basic form of predictive genetic information, insurers view genetic testing as a natural extension of the risk information that could be used in the underwriting process.[43] Opponents of genetic testing argue that genetic tests, other than those which test for and

---

[37] *AHEC, supra,* note 3 at 305.
[38] Bartha M. Knoppers et al., "Genetics and Life Insurance in Canada: Points to Consider", Canadian Medical Association Journal 170 (9), April 27, 2004 at 1 [*Knoppers*].
[39] *CHRA, supra,* note 4, ss. 20-22.
[40] *AHEC, supra,* note 3 at 346.
[41] *Godard, supra,* note 22 at S124.
[42] *AHEC, supra,* note 3 at 338.
[43] *Ibid.,* at 334.

diagnose dominant single-gene disorders, are not yet accurate, reliable or currently available on the market and therefore can rarely be used effectively in risk assessment.[44] There is also concern that permitting insurers to collect and use genetic test information may deter employees from undergoing tests which might enable early detection and treatment of disease, or from participating in genetic research, fearing that insurance companies may reject their applications for insurance.[45]

The Supreme Court of Canada has ruled that restricting disability insurance benefits is discriminatory. In *Battlefords & District Co-operative Ltd. v. Gibbs*,[46] the insurance company terminated the benefits of an employee receiving disability payments due to mental illness. The policy required benefits to cease after two years if the employee was not institutionalized, even if the employee was permanently unable to work. However, employees suffering physical disabilities continued to receive benefits until age 65. The Court determined that the mental and physical disability schemes were designed for the same purpose, thus, limiting the employee's entitlement to benefits because of her type of disability was discriminatory and contravened the human rights code. This decision suggests that in the context of genetic predispositions or disease, a disability insurer would likely be prohibited from discriminating against an employee currently enrolled in a disability plan on the basis of genetic status. How the Court would rule in a case where the employee was not yet a holder of such a policy is less clear, however, human rights legislation clearly indicates that discrimination in relation to insurance plans is not prohibited under its purview.

In the United States, at least 44 States have enacted specific legislation that regulates the use of genetic information by insurance companies and generally prohibits insurers from excluding applicants from coverage or raising premiums on the basis of genetic abnormalities. In 1996, the federal government introduced the *Health Insurance Portability and Accountability Act of 1996*, which includes protection against excluding an individual from group insurance because of genetic information, charging a higher premium to one individual than to others in group insurance, exclusions in a group health plan for a pre-existing condition to 12 months, as well as exclusions if the individual has been previously covered for that condition for 12 months or more. The Act also provides explicit provisions stating that

---

[44] *Supra*, note 24 at 2.
[45] *Godard, supra*, note 22 at S124, S130.
[46] [1996] 3 S.C.R. 566 (S.C.C.).

genetic information in the absence of a current diagnosis of illness shall not be considered a pre-existing condition.[47]

8.2.5 The Tension between the Potential Benefits and Harms of Genetic Testing

Genetic technology shows great potential for the prediction, diagnosis, treatment and prevention of diseases, however, the foregoing discussion indicates that threats to genetic privacy and risk of discrimination in employment and insurance could inhibit an employee from undergoing tests and treatment, and could seriously undermine scientific progress and the potential to improve health and health care.[48]

Another salient issue involves balancing respect for individual autonomy and an employee's right *not* to know about a potential or pending disease, particularly where there is no cure or effective medical treatment, against an employer's right or duty to know the results of a genetic test. The matter is further complicated by the question as to whether a duty exists to inform biological relatives of the employee's test results, even though the employee may not want this information to be disclosed to his or her family members. However, one employee's test results could inadvertently affect the employability and insurability of a wide range of family members.[49]

Thus, Canada's laws are challenged to reconcile the potential conflict between individual privacy rights and public interests, including those of a family member, institutions, researchers, and perhaps the right of citizens to receive the health benefits from genetic testing.[50]

---

[47] *AHEC, supra,*, note 3 at 353, 354.
[48] *Oscapella, supra*, note 8 at 21, 29.
[49] *Ibid.*, at 22, 23.
[50] *Jones, supra*, note 24 at 16, 24.

9

Drug Testing & Privacy

9.1 DRUG TESTING

9.1.1 Introduction

Workplace alcohol and drug programs, in various forms, have been in place in Canada for over 25 years. Some have consisted solely of employee assistance programs, while others have been more comprehensive and have included the implementation of drug and alcohol testing policies.[1]

The implementation of drug testing policies by employers is felt to be justified due to the prevalence of drug use in the workplace and the serious consequences associated with such use, such as: accidents resulting in serious personal and property damage; excessive absenteeism giving rise to sick-leave benefits, insurance and compensation claims; loss of overall productivity and human potential; lower quality products and services; and increased corporate liability attributable to employee negligence and wrongdoing.[2] However, the implementation of such company policies have been heavily criticized by those who maintain that drug testing is an unwarranted intrusion into the employee's privacy. Consequently, there continue to be legal challenges to an employer's right to request these tests.[3]

---

[1] Roger K. MacDougall, *Canadian Workplace Privacy Rights–Alcohol and Drug Policy and Testing Issues: Development, Implementation and Legal Overview* (Ottawa: Canadian Bar Association-Continuing Legal Education Seminar, 1999) at 10. Since 1986, the number of Canadian companies which have instituted mandatory drug and alcohol testing has significantly increased both in the private and public sectors. Air Canada, Imperial Oil, the Ontario Racing Commission, the Toronto-Dominion Bank, Canadian National Railway, Canadian Pacific, and American Motors (Canada), are some of the employers who have introduced testing programs in their respective workplaces.

[2] B. Butler, *Alcohol and Drugs in the Workplace* (Markham: Butterworths, 1993) at 27.

[3] Roger K. MacDougall, *supra* note 1 at 10.

9.1.2 Is Drug Testing an Invasion of Privacy?

Policies of drug and alcohol testing are personally invasive in three distinct manners. First, routine drug tests are intrusive. The tests are often set up so that another person must accompany the employee so as to ensure there is no specimen tampering. Similarly, the requirement to remove one's outer garments and to urinate in a bathroom is degrading.

Second, the laboratory procedure itself is an invasion of an employee's privacy. Urinalysis reveals not only the presence of illegal drugs, but also the existence of many other physical and medical conditions, including pregnancy and/ or the genetic predisposition to disease.[4]

Third, the potential for false positive results due to human error in the labotatory is present. Frequently drug tests fail to distinguish between legal and illegal substances. For example, Depronil, a prescription drug used to treat Parkinson's disease, has shown up as an amphetamine on standard drug tests. Over-the-counter anti-inflammatory drugs like Ibuprofen have shown up positive on marihuana tests. Even the poppy seeds found in baked goods can produce a positive result for heroin.[5]

9.1.3 The American Approach

While presently there is no Canadian legislation providing for mandatory drug testing of employees, companies doing business in the U.S., may be obliged to respect U.S. legislation and policy and perform drug tests on their employees. For example, the Federal Highway Administration (FHWA) which regulates the motor carrier industry, has in place regulations requiring drug and alcohol testing of commercial motor vehicle drivers.[6] As of July 1, 1996, these regulations were extended to Canadian trucking

---

[4] For example, in 1988, the Washington, D.C. Police Department admitted it used urine samples collected for drug tests to screen female employees for pregnancy — without their knowledge or consent (See American Civil Liberties Union, News Release, "Privacy in America: Workplace Drug Testing," (1999), online: <http://www.aclu.org/library/pbr5.html>.

[5] *Ibid.*

[6] *Federal Motor Carrier Safety Regulations, Title 49 Code of Federal Regulations, Parts 40 and 382*, U.S. Department of Transportation, Federal Highway Administration. The workplace drug and alcohol policy and program is to consist of pre-employment drug testing as well as random drug and alcohol testing at a minimum annual rate of 25 per cent of the driver pool for alcohol and 50 per cent for drugs. Employers are responsible for complying with the regulations, including the testing requirements, and can not use a driver in cross-border work who is unqualified or in violation of these rules.

companies. Previously, there had been an exemption for Canadian carriers and drivers. This foreign carrier exemption was lifted when the Government of Canada announced in December 1994 that it would not be proceeding with similar legislation.[7]

An Interim Report issued in January 1999 by the Special Senate Committee on Transportation Safety and Security, recommended that Transport Canada reconsider its position and that the Canadian government should proceed to permit mandatory, random drug and alcohol testing in the transportation industry similar to United States legislation.[8] It remains to be seen if the government will act on this recommendation.

There have been cases in the United States which have ruled that mandatory urine testing of public sector employees is a violation of the constitution. Many state and federal courts have ruled that testing programs in public sector workplaces are unconstitutional if they are not based on reasonably based suspicion. Throughout the country, courts have struck down programs that randomly tested police officers, fire-fighters, teachers, civilian army employees, prison guards and employees of many federal agencies.[9]

In 1989, the United States Supreme Court ruled on the constitutionality of drug testing public sector employees. The court held that while urine tests are searches, a public sector employer may have the right to search an employee who is not a suspected drug user so long as an employee's Fourth Amendment right to privacy is outweighed by the government's interest in maintaining a drug-free workplace.[10]

With respect to United States private sector employees, it remains to be seen whether or not drug testing programs will be uniformly sanctioned by the courts. In most states, private sector employees have virtually no protection against drug testing's intrusion on their privacy unless they belong to a union that has negotiated the prohibition or restriction of workplace testing. One exception is California, in which the state constitution specifies a right to privacy that applies, not only to government action, but to actions by private business as well.[11]

---

[7] Nancy Holmes, *Drug Testing: Legal Implications*, (Research Branch: Law and Government Division, Library of Parliament, 1996) at 6.
[8] Recommendation 3 of the Interim Report issued on January 1999.
[9] *Department of Public Education – American Civil Liberties Union, Briefing Paper Number 5*, "Drug Testing in the Workplace," (23 Nov. 1992) online: <http://www.eff.org/pub/Privacy/Workplace/acludrugtestingworkplace.faq>.
[10] *Skinner v. Railway Labour Executives' Assn.*, 489 U.S. 602 (U.S. Cal., 1989).
[11] In addition to California, only a handful of other states have enacted protective legislation that restricts drug testing in the private workplace and gives employees

9.1.4 The Canadian Approach

There is no Canadian legislation dealing specifically with drug testing - either mandating it, or prohibiting it. There has been no decision from the Supreme Court of Canada addressing the question and cases from lower courts and administrative tribunals have varied considerably. As a result, there remains some level of uncertainty in the Canadian legal environment concerning company drug testing programs.

(a) The Charter of Rights and Freedoms

If a government institution has instituted a program requiring the mandatory testing of employees, any challenges to such a policy would likely be brought under sections 7 and 8 of the Charter.[12] Such challenges could also be based on section 15 which holds that every individual is equal before and under the law and has the right to the equal protection and equal benefit of the law without discrimination on the basis of race, national or ethnic origin, colour, religion, sex, age or *mental or physical disability*.[13]

---

some measure of protection from unfair and unreliable testing. The states of Montana, Iowa, Vermont and Rhode Island have banned all random or blanket drug testing of employees (i.e., testing without probable cause or reasonable suspicion), and Minnesota, Maine and Connecticut permit random testing only of employees in "safety-sensitive" positions. The laws in these states also mandate confirmatory testing, use of certified laboratories, confidentiality of test results and other procedural protections. These laws place significant limits on employers' otherwise unfettered authority to test and give employees the power to resist unwarranted invasions of privacy. Only in California, Massachusetts and New Jersey have the highest courts ruled out some forms of drug testing on state constitutional or statutory grounds. [See Department of Public Education — American Civil Liberties Union, Briefing Paper Number 5, "Drug Testing in the Workplace," (23 Nov. 1992) online: <http://www.eff.org/pub/Privacy/Workplace/acludrugtestingworkplace.faq>].

[12] The constitutionality of mandatory drug and/ or alcohol testing has been considered in *R. v. Chatham* (1985), 23 C.R.R. 344 (B.C. S.C.); *Jackson v. Joyceville Penitentiary*, [1990] 3 F.C. 55 (Fed. T.D.) in the context of drug testing regulations in penitentiaries and in impaired driving cases where is was held under section 7 that the non-consensual taking of an individual's bodily fluids infringes the security of the person. The taking of bodily samples has been held to constitute a seizure within the meaning of section 8 in *R. v. Dyment*, [1988] 2 S.C.R. 417 (S.C.C.).

[13] The same type of argument as used under the *Canadian Human Rights Act* (i.e., discrimination on the basis of "disability").

(b) *Canadian Human Rights Act*[14]

The *Canadian Human Rights Act* applies to all federal government departments, agencies, Crown corporations, and to businesses which fall under federal jurisdiction such as banks, airlines and railway companies. A 2002 policy statement issued by the Canadian Human Rights Commission states that under the Act, employee drug testing might be considered to be a discriminatory practice on the ground of disability. Furthermore, in the tribunal decision discussed below, it was held that as a blanket policy, mandatory urinalysis represents a major invasion of privacy in the employment field.[15]

Disability is defined in the Act as including any previous or existing dependence on alcohol or drugs.[16] Sections 7, 8 and 10 of the *Canadian Human Rights Act*, allow a federal employee who has been disciplined for testing positive in a drug test to file a complaint with the Commission alleging discrimination on the basis of disability.

Under the Act, an employer has a defence to a charge of discriminatory practice if they can show that the practice is justified as a "bona fide occupational requirement". In drug testing cases, the employer would have to demonstrate objectively that a "positive" test result indicated decreased ability to perform the job safely, efficiently and reliably, and, wherever possible, that assessments of capacity to perform were individualized.

In *Canadian Civil Liberties Assn. v. Toronto Dominion Bank*[17] the Toronto-Dominion Bank implemented a drug testing program which re-

---

[14] *Canadian Human Rights Act*, R.S.C. 1985, c. H-6.
[15] See *Canadian Civil Liberties Assn. v. Toronto Dominion Bank, infra* note 17.
[16] Section 25.
[17] (1994), 22 C.H.R.R. D/301 (Can. Human Rights Trib.), reversed (1996), (*sub nom. Canadian Human Rights Commission v. Toronto Dominion Bank*) 112 F.T.R. 127, 25 C.H.R.R. D/373 (Fed. T.D.), reversed (1998), 163 D.L.R. (4th) 193, 32 C.H.R.R. D/261 (Fed. C.A.). The test screened for cannabis (marihuana and hashish), cocaine and opiates (codeine, morphine and heroin). Where the first test is positive for an opiate and the employee has provided a credible medical explanation for taking prescription medications, the matter is reviewed with the Medical Director and the employee is usually given the benefit of the doubt. In the case of the finding of cocaine use, the employee's file is immediately transferred to a rehabilitation nurse for follow-up with that employee. In the case of a finding of cannabis, the employee is notified and advised that a second test will be necessary. If the second test is positive for cannabis then the employee is referred to a rehabilitation nurse and to an assessment centre. If the third test is positive, steps are taken to terminate the employment regardless of whether the

9.1.4(b) PRIVACY IN EMPLOYMENT

quired newly hired employees to undergo urine tests within 48 hours of being accepted for employment. This program was challenged by the Canadian Civil Liberties Association who argued that the program was discriminatory on the basis of disability under section 10 of the *Canadian Human Rights Act*.

The Canadian Human Rights Tribunal found that the drug testing policy of the TD bank did not discriminate against drug dependent persons pursuant to the *Canadian Human Rights Act*.[18] Relevant to the Tribunal's decision was the fact that the Bank's testing requirement was not a prerequisite for employment but rather came into effect only after a candidate had been hired. Since all prospective employees were notified of the requirement to submit to the drug test as a condition of employment, a failure to comply constituted a breach of a condition of employment, rather than discrimination. Moreover, the Bank's ultimate dismissal of an employee who failed to pass all three of the company's drug testing stages was based on a finding of persistent use of an illegal substance. Lastly, the Board held that any finding of drug dependency is one of diagnosis and not of perceived disability as contemplated under the *Canadian Human Rights Act*.

The Federal Court of Canada (Trial Division)[19] overturned this decision and found that the drug testing policy of the Bank did amount to discrimination under the Act. The Court held that the policy was indirectly discriminating in that while neutral on its face, it had a negative impact on drug-dependent persons, a subgroup protected by the human rights legislation. However, it was held that an employer may implement a drug testing policy if able to show that it is rationally connected to the employment and that reasonable steps have been taken to accommodate the complainant, short of undue hardship to the employer. In summary, the Trial Division held that where an employee has consented to a drug test and it is clear that the employer has implemented its policy as a condition of employment, it would be difficult to establish discrimination under section 10 of the *CHRA*.

The Bank appealed this decision to the Federal Court of Appeal.[20] In a 2:1 decision, the Court of Appeal held that the Bank could not justify testing in the circumstances. While the majority decision differed on whether the discrimination was direct or indirect, some of the key factors relevant to their determination were: the Bank had failed to make out the *bona fide* occupational defence; there was no evidence of a drug problem

---

employee's medical assessment indicates drug dependence or persistent casual use.

[18] *Toronto Dominion Bank, ibid.*
[19] *Canadian Civil Liberties Assn. v. Toronto Dominion Bank, supra,* note 17.
[20] *Ibid.*

in the workforce; the employer could not show that mandatory testing was the least intrusive reasonable method to assess job performance; and the Bank failed to prove that employee work performance was affected by drugs. Interestingly, two of the three justices likely would have upheld testing in the appropriate circumstances in safety sensitive industries.

This case placed importance on the distinction between adverse impact and direct discrimination as well as the meaning of reasonable accommodation to the point of undue hardship within the context of the *bona fide* occupational requirement exception.[21] However, *Bill S-5* in 1998 has since removed the word "reasonable" and restricted the meaning of "undue hardship" to considerations of health, safety and cost.[22] Furthermore, a recent Supreme Court of Canada judgment eliminated the adverse impact/direct impact dichotomy.[23]

The general principles which emerge from decisions under the Human Rights regime are that an employer has a right to ensure that its business operations are conducted safely, and a corresponding right to assess whether employees are incapable of performing their essential duties. This right generally outweighs an employee's privacy right in cases where an employee is hired to work in a safety sensitive position. For example, in *Entrop v. Imperial Oil Ltd.*[24] the employer's (Imperial Oil) drug testing program was alleged to discriminate on the basis of "handicap" under the *Ontario Human Rights Code*.[25] Imperial Oil's Alcohol and Drug Policy subjected all job applicants to a urinalysis test for drugs as a condition of employment.

---

[21] For further information on the issue of what is reasonable accommodation to the point of undue hardship see: *O'Malley v. Simpsons-Sears Ltd.*, (sub nom. *Ontario Human Rights Commission v. Simpsons-Sears Ltd.*), [1985] 2 S.C.R. 536 (S.C.C.); *Renaud v. Central Okanagan School District No. 23*, (sub nom. *Central Okanagan School District No. 23 v. Renaud*), [1992] 2 S.C.R. 970 (S.C.C.); *Chambly (Commission scolaire régionale) c. Bergevin*, (sub nom. *Commission scolaire régionale de Chambly v. Bergevin*), [1994] 2 S.C.R. 525(S.C.C.); *Central Alberta Dairy Pool v. Alberta (Human Rights Commission)*, [1990] 2 S.C.R. 489 (S.C.C.).

[22] See *CHRA* s. 15(2).

[23] See *British Columbia (Public Service Employee Relations Commission) v. B.C.G.E.U.* (1999), [1999] S.C.J. No. 46, 1999 CarswellBC 1907 (S.C.C.).

[24] There were a series of human rights adjudication decisions on this matter culminating in *Entrop v. Imperial Oil Ltd.* (1996), 24 C.C.E.L. (2d) 122 (Ont. Bd. of Inquiry), affirmed (1998), 35 C.C.E.L. (2d) 56 (Ont. Div. Ct.), leave to appeal allowed (1998), 1998 CarswellOnt 1955 (Ont. C.A.), reversed (2000), 189 D.L.R. (4th) 14 (Ont. C.A.). This was the first decision in Ontario in the area of substance abuse testing.

[25] R.S.O. 1990, c. H.19.

9.1.4(b)   PRIVACY IN EMPLOYMENT

Any employees wishing to work in safety sensitive positions were also required to undergo drug testing in order to be certified for such work. Furthermore, as a condition of employment, employees could be subjected to random drug and alcohol testing. In addition to being tested, prospective and current employees in safety-sensitive positions were placed under a continuing obligation to disclose to management whether they have, or have ever had, a substance abuse problem or have received treatment or counselling for such a problem.

The Ontario Human Rights Board held that Imperial Oil has a right to ensure that its business operations are conducted safely, and a corresponding right to assess whether employees are incapable of performing their essential duties. For safety sensitive positions, Imperial Oil was also found to have the right to assess whether its employees are free from impairment on the job, whether by alcohol, drug abuse, or otherwise. However, while freedom from impairment of drugs and alcohol is a *bona fide* occupational requirement, it was held that Imperial Oil's Policy overreached this legitimate goal. It was further held that drug testing for cause, post-incident, certification into safety sensitive positions or post-reinstatement reasons may be upheld if testing is only one component of the overall assessment of abuse.[26]

The decision of the Board of Inquiry was upheld on appeal to the Ontario Divisional Court, but on further appeal to the Ontario Court of Appeal, the Board's decision was reversed in part. The appeal dealt with the issue of whether the Board of Inquiry had jurisdiction to expand the scope of its inquiry to include a determination as to whether Imperial's drug testing policy violated the *Ontario Human Rights Code*. The Court of Appeal ruled that the Board should not have expanded its inquiry to include an analysis of whether drug testing as well as alcohol testing, breaches the *Human Rights Code*. Despite this ruling, however, Laskin J.A. did examine the issue of whether Imperial's drug testing policy violated the Code.

Laskin J.A. applied the new three-step test developed by the Supreme Court of Canada in *British Columbia (Public Service Employee Relations Commission) v. B.C.G.S.E.U.* (1999), 176 D.L.R (4th) 1 (S.C.C.), (referred to by Laskin J.A. and herein as "*Meiorin*"). The test adopted by the Supreme Court was designed to eliminate the necessity for an inquiry into whether a particular type of discrimination is "direct" or "adverse effect" discrimi-

---

[26] *Entrop v. Imperial Oil Ltd.* (1998), 35 C.C.E.L. (2d) 56 (Ont. Div. Ct.), leave to appeal allowed (1998), 1998 CarswellOnt 1955 (Ont. C.A.), reversed (2000), 189 D.L.R. (4th) 14 (Ont. C.A.). This case was appealed by Imperial Oil to the Ontario Divisional Court where the Court decided that it would not interfere with the adjudicator's rulings. Leave to appeal this decision was granted by the Ontario Court of Appeal — (May 12, 1998), Doc. CA M22074 (Ont. C.A.).

nation. This line of inquiry was seen by courts as being increasingly problematic and given to inconsistent and arbitrary remedies, depending upon the characterization of the discrimination.

In *Meiorin*, McLachlin J. proposed the following test, which can be used by an employer to justify an impugned employment standard as being a *bona fide* occupational requirement ("BFOR"). By establishing, on the balance of probabilities, that:

(1) The employer adopted the standard for a purpose rationally connected to the performance of the job;

(2) The employer adopted the standard in an honest and good faith belief that it was necessary to the fulfilment of that legitimate work-related purpose; and

(3) The standard is reasonably necessary to the accomplishment of that legitimate work-related purpose. To show that the standard is reasonably necessary, it must be demonstrated that it is impossible to accommodate individual employees sharing the characteristics of the claimant without imposing undue hardship upon the employer,[27]

the employer can justify the impugned employment standard as a BFOR. Applying this analysis to Imperial Oil, Laskin J.A. held that the company's alcohol testing policy was a BFOR. However, its drug testing policy did not pass the test set out in *Meiorin*.

Laskin J.A. held that substance abusers are handicapped within the meaning of the *Ontario Human Rights Code* and are therefore entitled to freedom from discrimination in their workplace based on their handicap. Since perceived as well as actual substance abuse is included in the definition of "handicap" under the Code, anyone testing positive under the alcohol and drug testing provisions of Imperial Oil's policy is entitled to the protection of section 5. The sanctions imposed by the company applied to any person testing positive in an alcohol or drug test and were *prima facie* discriminatory. As a result, Imperial Oil bore the onus of proving that the testing and the sanctions imposed for testing positive are BFORs.

The Court of Appeal held that Imperial Oil had adopted a drug and alcohol testing policy for a purpose rationally connected to the job, and that Imperial Oil did, in fact, have an honest and good faith belief that its policy was necessary to accomplish the company's purpose. Therefore Imperial Oil met the first two steps of the *Meiorin* test. However, with respect to the

---

[27] *British Columbia (Public Service Employee Relations Commission) v. B.C.G.E.U.* (1999), (sub nom. *British Columbia (Public Service Employee Relations Commission) v. B.C.G.S.E.U.*) 176 D.L.R. (4th) 1 (S.C.C.), at pp. 24-25.

third stage of the test, whether the means used to accomplish the purpose were reasonably necessary, Laskin J.A. found Imperial Oil's policy deficient.

Dealing first with the issue of drug testing, Laskin J.A. held that the drugs listed in Imperial Oil's policy have the capacity to impair job performance and that urinalysis is a reliable method of showing the presence of drugs or drug metabolites in a person's body. However, he held that:

> ... drug testing suffers from one fundamental flaw. It cannot measure present impairment. A positive drug test shows only past drug use. It cannot show how much was used or when it was used. Thus, the Board found that a positive drug test provides no evidence of impairment or likely impairment on the job. It does not demonstrate that a person is incapable of performing the essential duties of the position. The Board also found on the evidence that no tests currently exist to accurately assess the effect of drug use on job performance and that drug testing programs have not been shown to be effective in reducing drug use, work accidents or work performance problems. On these findings, random drug testing for employees in safety-sensitive positions cannot be justified as reasonably necessary to accomplish Imperial Oil's legitimate goal of a safe workplace free of impairment.

Laskin J.A. also found that the sanction provisions of Imperial Oil's drug testing policy were too severe, as they mandated automatic termination for all employees after a single positive test. Imperial Oil had failed to demonstrate why it could not tailor its sanctions to accommodate individual capabilities without incurring undue hardship.

Laskin J.A. found that the provisions for random alcohol testing stand on a different footing. Breathalyzer tests can show present impairment. Expert evidence before the Board confirmed the reliability and utility of breathalyzers to measure alcohol impairment. The Board relied on evidence to the effect that increased supervision of employees by properly trained personnel would be more likely to detect impairment on the job. However, random alcohol testing will not pass the third step of the *Meiorin* test unless the employer meets its duty to accommodate the needs of those who test positive. As a result, Laskin J.A. set aside the Board's conclusion that random alcohol testing for employees breached the Code, and held instead that this type of testing is a BFOR, provided that the sanctions imposed for an employee testing positive are tailored to the employee's circumstances.

Laskin J.A. also held that requiring an employee to disclose a past substance abuse problem, no matter how far in the past, is an unreasonable requirement. The Board found, on evidence before it, that a point can be reached by former substance abusers when the risk of relapse or recurrence is small. The Board found the cut-off point to be five to six years of successful remission. In applying its policy of relocation and reassignment of individuals identifying themselves as former substance abusers, without consideration of the length of time the individual had been drug or alcohol free, Imperial Oil's treatment of the employee was unjustified. In conclusion, Laskin J.A. ruled that random alcohol testing for employees in safety sensitive positions is a BFOR, provided that the sanctions for an employee testing positive are tailored to the employee's circumstances.

As a result of the Court of Appeal ruling in *Entrop*, and, in particular Laskin J.A.'s *obiter* comments respecting the efficacy of random drug testing, the status of drug testing in the workplace under Ontario human rights legislation remains somewhat unclear.

A recent arbitration decision reinforces the differing approach to mandatory workplace drug and alcohol testing in Canada as opposed to the United States.[28] While federal legislation requires certain types of United States employees to undergo that kind of testing, the Canadian approach involves a case-by-case balancing of the employer's interest in implementing such a regime against the intrusion into the employees' privacy that is inherent in the testing process itself.

The company, Bulk Systems, was acquired by Trimac in 1990. Trimac is a publicly-traded Canadian company, headquartered in Calgary, Alberta, with operations throughout North America. Bulk Systems, as with the other Trimac companies, utilized Trimac equipment, policies, insurance, operating authorities, accounting, human resource, pension and training system. Safety rules and safety training were structured on a company-wide basis. Given the homogeneity of the Trimac organization it is not surprising that there is a single drug and alcohol policy company-wide in Canada and a parallel policy in the United States. This policy was amended in 1996 to incorporate mandatory random drug and alcohol testing for its drivers to reflect the statutory regime in the United States (where mandatory drug and alcohol testing of transport drivers is required by federal law and where the parent company has sizeable operations). No such regime exists in Canada.

The Transport and Communications union challenged the application of the mandatory random drug testing policy to Bulk Systems' drivers whose work was confined to Canada. The union argued that there was no clear provision for drug and alcohol testing in the collective agreements covering those drivers, nor was there a legal requirement that they be tested. Even if the company could impose a drug and alcohol testing policy without clear contractual or statutory authority, the union argued that a "balancing of interests" test applied.

---

[28] *Trimac Transportation Services - Bulk Systems v. T.C.U.* (1999), 88 L.A.C. (4th) 237 (Can. Arb. Bd.).

9.1.4(b)

The arbitrator found that the company's mandatory random drug and alcohol testing program was unenforceable under the collective agreement. Although the grievance was decided by the arbitrator within the parameters of the collective agreement, the issue of compliance with human rights legislation, raised by the parties, was also addressed in the arbitrator's reasons. The company attempted to distinguish its case from that of *Entrop*, on the basis that the policy under attack in that case targeted persons with a handicap, while Bulk Systems' policy was aimed at all its drivers and had the legitimate business purpose of preventing drivers who have drugs or alcohol in their systems from reporting to work. The company argued that this type of "adverse effect" discrimination on individuals with a drug or alcohol addiction was accommodated by the company to the point of undue hardship. However, the arbitrator held that the company failed to discharge the onus upon it of establishing that its policy was rationally connected to its legitimate business interest and that it had also failed to establish any pre-existing experience or incidents within the particular bargaining unit which would support the necessity for mandatory random drug testing. Following the line of reasoning in *Entrop*, the arbitrator held that the urinalysis mechanism used to detect drug use does not establish whether an employee is under the influence at work.

The 2002 Federal Human Rights Commission, after public consultation and a review of the jurisprudence, released a comprehensive policy indicating the types of testing that will be considered permissible. The Policy states:

> Because they cannot be established as bona fide occupational requirements, the following types of testing are not acceptable:
> - Pre-employment drug testing
> - Pre-employment alcohol testing
> - Random drug testing
> - Random alcohol testing of employees in non-safety-sensitive positions.

The following types of testing may be included in a workplace drug- and alcohol-testing program, but only if an employer can demonstrate that they are *bona fide* occupational requirements:

> - Random alcohol testing of employees in safety sensitive positions. Alcohol testing has been found to be a reasonable requirement because alcohol testing can indicate actual impairment of ability to perform or fulfill the essential duties or requirements of the job. Random drug testing is prohibited because, given its technical limitations, drug testing can only detect the presence of drugs and not if or when an employee may have been impaired by drug use.

- Drug or alcohol testing for "reasonable cause" or "post-accident," e.g. where there are reasonable grounds to believe there is an underlying problem of substance abuse or where an accident has occurred due to impairment from drugs or alcohol, provided that testing is a part of a broader program of medical assessment, monitoring and support.

- Periodic or random testing following disclosure of a current drug or alcohol dependency or abuse problem may be acceptable if tailored to individual circumstances and as part of a broader program of monitoring and support. Usually, a designated rehabilitation provider will determine whether follow-up testing is necessary for a particular individual.

- Mandatory disclosure of present or past drug or alcohol dependency or abuse may be permissible for employees holding safety-sensitive positions, within certain limits, and in concert with accommodation measures. Generally, employees not in safety-sensitive positions should not be required to disclose past alcohol or drug problems.

In the limited circumstances where testing is justified, employees who test positive must be accommodated to the point of undue hardship. The *Canadian Human Rights Act* requires individualized or personalized accommodation measures. Policies that result in the employee's automatic loss of employment, reassignment, or that impose inflexible reinstatement conditions without regard for personal circumstances are unlikely to meet this requirement. Accommodation should include the necessary support to permit the employee to undergo treatment or a rehabilitation program, and consideration of sanctions less severe than dismissal.

The policy continues by explaining in what circumstances an employer would be relieved of the duty to accommodate.

(c) Arbitration

If there is no collective agreement which addresses the issue of employee drug testing, management may identify the establishment of a policy as a matter for collective bargaining or may attempt to unilaterally impose the policy.[29] Arbitration cases typically centre on the ability of the employer to unilaterally impose a management rule dealing with drug testing of employees. A drug testing policy will only be enforceable if it satisfies the following conditions: it must be clear, unequivocal and consistently enforced by the company from the time it is introduced; it must not be unreasonable or inconsistent with the collective agreement; and the policy must

---

[29] B. Butler, *supra* note 2 at 115.

be brought to the attention of the employees with clear explanation as to the consequences of a breach of the rule.[30]

While each of these factors can be expected to be looked at in an arbitration case, the primary focus is the "reasonableness" of the rule. In considering the reasonableness of implementing a mandatory drug testing policy, the "balance of interest" test, developed in *KVP*[31] is applied (i.e., balancing the right of an employee to privacy against the right of and responsibility of an employer to ensure that his or her employees are safe and unimpaired and the public is safe). The test is a function of risk assessment. For instance, the higher the workplace risk the more reasonable it is to justify an invasion of the employee's privacy by demanding drug and alcohol testing, even on a random basis. Similarly, where the workplace risk is low, fewer forms of testing will be justifiable or none at all where there is insufficient evidence of a problem.

For example, in *Provincial-American Truck Transporters v. Teamsters Union, Local 880*[32] the collective agreement specifically gave the company the right to request medical examinations. Citing *Canadian Pacific Ltd. v. U.T.U.*,[33] the arbitrator analogized drug testing to employee searches and broadly interpreted the provision relating to medical examination to encompass drug and alcohol testing. The "balancing of interests" test was applied as follows:

> ... If there is a reason to demand a test, then a test can be demanded. That is, if a particular employee gives the company reasonable grounds for believing that his/ her fitness to perform the job safely is impaired by use of alcohol or drugs, then the company should be able to test as part of its rights under art. 13. If mandatory universal testing is to be justified, absent a specific term allowing it, then there should at least be evidence of a drug and/or alcohol problem in the work-place which cannot be combated in some less invasive way. In this case we have no such evidence.[34]

Upon application of the above test, the arbitrator ruled that the employer's policy was unreasonable within the meaning of the *KVP* test. The company had not produced any evidence demonstrating any adverse impact on the company's operations by reason of substance abuse among employees, nor was there any evidence of problems regarding impaired drivers

---

[30] *Lumber & Sawmill Workers' Union, Local 2537 v. KVP Co.* (1965), 16 L.A.C. 73 (Ont. Arb. Bd.).
[31] *Ibid.*
[32] (1991), 18 L.A.C. (4th) 412 (Ont. Arb. Bd.).
[33] (1987), 31 L.A.C. (3d) 179 (Can. Arb. Bd.).
[34] *Ibid.* at 425.

which were not being adequately addressed by the existing rules and regime of physical examinations.[35]

Drug and alcohol testing of employees has generally been upheld in the context of safety-sensitive jobs, post-accident investigations, reasonable cause, certification into safety sensitive positions and return to duty after time away from work. In order to successfully implement such a policy, the employer must have a sufficient rational. The employer must show that drug and alcohol use in the workplace is a significant issue and/or the conduct of an employee is such as to give reasonable grounds that the employee is impaired. Finally, any policy must be tailored to the individual workplace; the problems therein and the collective bargaining regime in place.[36]

In *Canadian Pacific Ltd. v. U.T.U.*[37] an employee had been charged with cultivation and possession of marihuana plants. The employee, a conductor, when asked by CP to submit to a drug test, refused and was dismissed. It was held that an employer has a right to require an employee to undergo a fitness examination, including a drug test, when the employer is a public carrier, the employee's duties are inherently safety sensitive and the employer has reasonable grounds to believe that the employee may be impaired while on duty or subject to duty. The arbitrator found that the condition must be seen as implicit in the contract of employment, absent any express provisions to the contrary.

In *Esso Petroleum Canada v. C.E.P., Local 614*,[38] like the *Entrop* case above, involved Imperial Oil's alcohol and drug employee policy which required random alcohol and drug testing, mandatory medical examinations, obligatory self-disclosure of present and past substance abuse problems and listed medications, and searches of employees working in jobs determined to be safety sensitive. The policy also provided for drug and alcohol testing of all employees for reasonable cause and after a significant accident. The union filed a policy grievance contesting the implementation of this policy at the Ioco refinery near Vancouver.

The arbitrator stated that "neither the managerial rights of the employer nor the rights of privacy of the employee are absolute". In examining the reasonableness of implementing the drug testing policy, the Board determined that the company should have first implemented alternative measures to combat the problem such as enacting rules of conduct for the workplace,

---

[35] *Ibid.*
[36] Roger K. MacDougall, *supra* note 1 at 19.
[37] *Supra*, note 33.
[38] (1994), 56 L.A.C. (4th) 440 (B.C. Arb. Bd.).

supervision, and evaluation measures or employee performance testing.[39] Upon balancing the interests of the employee's right to privacy and the employer's right to a safe working environment, it was determined that the policy could not be upheld as there was no evidence of a problem specific to that workplace to justify such action.[40]

The Board did find, however, that the implementation of the following rules was reasonable: prohibitions against use, possession, distribution, offering or sale of illicit drugs or alcohol while on company premises, prohibition against intentional misuse of prescribed medications while on company premises, prohibition against being unfit for scheduled work because of use of alcohol or illicit drugs, prohibition for employees in safety sensitive positions from consuming any alcoholic or illicit drugs during working hours, whether on or off company premises (including mealtimes, breaks, paid or unpaid) and requiring them to notify management if they have a current substance abuse problem. Furthermore, it was determined that mandatory testing of all employees on the basis of reasonable and probable cause and after a significant work accident, or near miss was acceptable.[41]

In *Sarnia Cranes*[42] a contractor to Imperial Oil had implemented an alcohol and drug testing policy. The Board held all forms of testing to be unjustified. No evidence was shown of problems with drug or alcohol use in the workplace. Furthermore, the company failed the *KVP* test since the risk of discipline/ discharge was unclear and was not communicated to employees[43] and the contractor did not first consider less intrusive methods of problem detection.[44] Interestingly, the Board held that the testing itself was unreasonable under the *KVP* test since a drug test cannot measure impairment and there had been no evidence of drug or alcohol problems in the workplace.[45]

In contrast, the Alberta Board in *Procor*[46] ruled that the testing of an employee who was convicted of possession of marihuana was reasonable,

---

[39] *Ibid.* at 448.
[40] *Ibid.* at 441.
[41] See *National Automobile, Aerospace, Transportation and General Workers Union of Canada v. Canadian National Railway Company*, Labour Arbitration News, September/ October, 2000 (M. Picher).
[42] *I.U.O.E, Local 793 v. Sarnia Cranes Ltd.*, [1999] O.L.R.B. Rep. 479 (Ont. L.R.B.).
[43] *Ibid.* at para 179.
[44] *Ibid.* at para 213.
[45] *Ibid.* at para. 56.
[46] *Procor Sulphur Services v. C.E.P., Local 57* (1998), 79 L.A.C. (4th) 341 (Alta. Arb. Bd.).

despite the fact that the company had no formal testing policy and had never previously tested any employee. The Board held that the employer was justified in requiring testing since the employee was in a safety sensitive position and had been in the possession of a substantial amount of marihuana.

10

Disclosure of Employee Information

10.1 DISCLOSURE TO UNIONS

Privacy in the workplace also imposes an obligation on employers to keep employee information confidential. In fact, certain employers have begun refusing to communicate employee related information. Sometimes, however, the employer's obligations to safeguard its employees' information may be tempered.

For example, in *H.R.E.U., Local 448 v. Millcroft Inn Ltd.*[1] the union brought an application to the Ontario Labour Relations Board for consent to prosecute the employer on the basis that the employer's refusal to provide the addresses and telephone numbers of its employees was a flagrant violation of the *Labour Relations Act, 1995*, S.O. 1995, c. 1. Arbitrator Christopher J. Albertyn upheld his decision of August 25, 2000 and ordered the employer to provide the union with the names, addresses and telephone numbers of the employees in the bargaining unit represented by the union. However, the application for consent to prosecute the employer was dismissed.

The *Millcroft* decision was followed in *O.S.S.T.F., District 25 v. Ottawa-Carleton District School Board.*[2] In this case, the employer was governed, not only by the provisions of the *Labour Relations Act*, but also by the *Municipal Freedom to Information and Protection of Privacy Act*. Interestingly, an earlier decision by the Ontario Information and Privacy Commissioner upheld the employer's decision to refuse to disclose personal information (the home addresses and telephone numbers) of its employees to the union who had requested the information. The Information and Privacy Commissioner ruled that the union's status as the collective bargaining agent was an irrelevant consideration in deciding whether or not the release of the information would be an unreasonable invasion of privacy under the privacy legislation. However, the arbitrator in *O.S.S.T.F., District 25 v. Ottawa-Carleton District School Board* (who was the same arbitrator who heard the *Millcroft* matter) determined that the request by the union for the

---

[1] (2000), [2000] O.L.R.D. No. 2581, 2000 CarswellOnt 3073 (Ont. L.R.B.) 7 online QL (LRBD).

[2] (2001), [2001] O.L.R.D. No. 4575, 2001 CarswellOnt 4902 (Ont. L.R.B.).

employees' home addresses and telephone numbers had to be obeyed by the employer in order to comply with section 70 of the *Labour Relations Act*. Section 70 states:

> No employer or employers' organization and no person acting on behalf of an employer or an employers' organization shall participate in or interfere with the formation, selection or administration of a trade union or the representation of employees by a trade union or contribute financial or other support to a trade union, but nothing in this section shall be deemed to deprive an employer of the employer's freedom to express views so long as the employer does not use coercion, intimidation, threats, promises or undue influence.

In trying to reconcile his decision to the earlier decision of the Information and Privacy Commissioner, the arbitrator determined that the Commissioner erred by failing to appreciate the significance of the union's statutory role as agent and representative of the employees in a bargaining unit.[3]

In *Society of Professional Engineers & Associates v. Atomic Energy of Canada Ltd.*,[4] the Society of Professional Engineers and Associates brought an application to the Canada Industrial Relations Board seeking an order that Atomic Energy of Canada Limited provide requested information regarding salary increases and promotions which had been given to certain employees in July 1999. The Board granted the application and ordered the employer to provide the union with the names of all relevant bargaining unit members, together with their level and salary.

---

[3] A similar case with a similar result, but involving the interplay between the federal *Public Service Staff Relations Act* and the federal *Privacy Act* is *P.S.A.C. v. Canada (Treasury Board)* (April 26, 1996), Doc. 161-2-791, 169-2-584, [1996] C.P.S.S.R.B. No. 30 (Can. P.S.S.R.B.). In this case, the Canada Public Service Staff Relations Board held that the release of the home addresses and telephone numbers to the union would be an allowable disclosure of personal information under the *Privacy Act* because the Board determined that the information would be used for a consistent purpose (section 8(2)(a)) to that purpose for which it was collected in the first place. See also *Societé canadienne des postes c. S.P.C.* (January 31, 1995), Bergeron Arb. (Can. Arb. Bd.) and *Union of Canadian Correctional Officers c. Conseil du Trésor*, 2002 PSSRB 58 (Can. P.S.S.R.B.). The same result is found in the Alberta case of *U.F.C.W., Local 401 v. Economic Development Edmonton* (2002), [2002] A.L.R.B.R. No. 41, 2002 CarswellAlta 1031 (Alta. L.R.B.), application for stay denied (2002), [2002] A.J. No. 800, 2002 CarswellAlta 799 (Alta. Q.B.). See also *Northwest Territories v. Union of Northern Workers* (2001), [2001] N.W.T.J. No. 24, 2001 CarswellNWT 29 (N.W.T. S.C.).

[4] [2001] C.I.R.B.D. No. 7, [2001] C.I.R.B. No. 110, 2001 CarswellNat 3651 (C.I.R.B.).

A decision by the Privacy Commissioner of Canada emphasizes that an employer's disclosure of an employee's personal information to his or her union requires the consent or implied consent of the employee prior to disclosure. In one case, an airport authority employee complained that her employer had disclosed her personal information to three third parties without her consent. The complainant had initially requested access to certain information from her employer but was subsequently denied access. The employer then sent copies of her request to two union representatives and the coordinator of employee relations at the airport without her consent. The Commissioner determined that had the employee informed the union of the request for information from her employer, the forwarding of the request would have been valid on the basis of implied consent. However, as the employee had the right to act without union intervention, the disclosure of her personal information to the union without her consent was not acceptable.[5]

10.2 DISCLOSURE TO BOARDS/TRIBUNALS/COURTS

In *Simons v. Prince Edward Island (Workers' Compensation Board)*[6] the Prince Edward Island Court of Appeal ruled that the Worker's Compensation Board did not violate worker's privacy rights when it sent workers' medical information to consultants for assessment. The records were sent without the workers' consent or knowledge. To this end, the Court of Appeal cautioned that informing the workers should be discouraged because "a person who applies for benefits necessarily lowers his or her expectation of privacy in respect of his or her medical records . . .". In the Court's opinion, a worker's privacy interests had to give way to the Board's mandate of investigating and examining the legitimacy of one's entitlement.

In a similar complaint to the Privacy Commissioner of Canada, an employee alleged that a telecommunications company had inappropriately disclosed personal medical information about her to the Worker's Compensation Board without her consent and had then initiated a claim for compensation on behalf of the complainant. The company claimed that the disclosure was required pursuant to provincial workers' compensation legislation and that in accordance with the privacy legislation, the information had not been disclosed for purposes other than those for which it had been collected. The Commissioner held that although the employer had released the complainant's information to the Board without her consent, it had done so in compliance with provincial statute, thereby exempting the employer

---

[5] Privacy Commissioner of Canada, November 5 2001, Summary #20.
[6] (2000), 2000 CarswellPEI 47 (P.E.I. C.A.).

from the requirement to seek her consent prior to the disclosures. The Commissioner did determine, however, that the company did not have in place any policies or staff training materials pertaining to the handling of employee information and recommended that the company take steps to implement the necessary policies and materials.[7]

The Privacy Commissioner of Canada has determined that under the *Canada Labour Code* and section 7(3)(c) of *PIPEDA*, arbitrators have the jurisdiction to compel the production of information at arbitration hearings. An employee of a company that produces nuclear technology filed a complaint against her employer for allegedly disclosing her personal information when she appeared as a witness for a grievor in an arbitration hearing between another employee and the company. The complainant claimed that two of her performance appraisals were tendered as evidence as a means to discredit her as a witness, and that her personal information had been released inappropriately. The company argued that under *PIPEDA*, the arbitrator had jurisdiction to allow for the introduction of the performance appraisals and that the appraisals were used solely within the context of an arbitration hearing. Moreover, the appraisals were disclosed only to the arbitrator, the complainant, and the lawyer who represented the grievor's union. The Commissioner held that under the *Canada Labour Code*, arbitrators have the jurisdiction to compel the production of information and that the disclosure of the appraisals was permissible according to section 7(3)(c) of *PIPEDA*, as it was made pursuant to an "order made by a person with jurisdiction to compel the production of information". The arbitrator's allowance of the appraisals as an exhibit qualified as an order as per section 7(3)(c).[8]

Pursuant to the rules of court in Quebec, the Privacy Commissioner of Canada has confirmed that if a plaintiff introduces evidence that the defendant intends to question at trial, the issue must be raised in discovery. Following a trial in a Quebec Court involving a class action lawsuit by a consumer group, a former employee of a telecommunications company who had offered to testify complained that his former employer had disclosed the reasons for his dismissal to a third party. The employer conceded that it had disclosed this information in discovery and contended that it had the right to do so since the disclosure pertained to litigation in a court proceeding in which the company was defending its interests. In this case, the Commissioner held that because the employer did intend to question the consumer group's material that was based on the complainant's statements, the employer was required to produce the proper evidence. In producing the

---

[7] Privacy Commissioner of Canada, July 11 2003, Summary #191.
[8] Privacy Commissioner of Canada, August 1 2003, Summary #198.

DISCLOSURE OF EMPLOYEE INFORMATION 10.2

affidavit regarding the appraisals, the employer was acting in accordance with the section 7(3)(c) exception in *PIPEDA* which allows for disclosure without an individuals' knowledge or consent where the disclosure is required to comply with the rules of court relating to the production of records.[9]

Certain provincial labour statutes also grant arbitrators the express power to order pre-hearing disclosure of documents containing the personal information of employees.[10] In *Toronto District School Board and C.U.P.E., Local 4400*,[11] the arbitrator held that at the pre-hearing stage, all documents in the parties' possession which have a semblance of relevance ought to be disclosed or at least identified where privilege applies. In this case, the employer filed grievances against the union claiming that the union had violated the collective agreement and workplace policy by distributing a partisan political message using the employer's email system. At the hearing, the employer made a preliminary motion to compel the union to produce certain documents prior to the hearing. The arbitrator ruled that all documents which are arguably or seemingly relevant, or have a semblance of relevance must be disclosed prior to the hearing at the request of the opposing party, and that once a general request for production is made, all documents relating to any matter in issue that is or has been in the possession, control or power of the opposing party must be disclosed, including documents for which privilege is claimed. In circumstances involving sensitive information such as medical records, an arbitrator has ruled that strict rules of confidentiality and relevance apply in order to protect a grievor's privacy. A Vancouver legal secretary, who left her job with the British Columbia Crown Attorney's office in 2002 following a reprimand regarding her job performance, applied for short-term illness and injury plan benefits on the grounds that she suffered from post-traumatic stress disorder, panic disorder, and major depressive disorder. When the government rejected her application on the basis that there was no evidence that her condition prevented her from working, the employee's union filed a grievance on her behalf and she produced a report from her psychiatrist which confirmed her illnesses and indicated that she could not deal with adversarial and confrontational situations.

The employer applied for pre-hearing disclosure of the psychiatrist's notes and report, in addition to records from her treating physicians and her

---

[9] Privacy Commissioner of Canada, March 16 2003, Summary #143.
[10] Ontario *Labour Relations Act, 1995*, S.O. 1995, c. 1, Sched. A, s. 48(12)(b); British Columbia *Labour Relations Code*, R.S.B.C. 1996, c. 244, s.82(2); Manitoba *Labour Relations Act*, R.S.M. 1987, c. L10 (s. 120(e)); *Canada Labour Code*, R.S.C. 1985, c. L-2 (ss. 60(1)(a), 16(f.1)).
[11] (2002), 109 L.A.C. (4th) 20 (Ont. Arb. Bd.).

Government Employees' Health Services file. In balancing the grievor's right to privacy against the employer's entitlement to a fair hearing, the arbitrator ruled that since the employee put her mental state at issue in a grievance, her medical records should be disclosed but only if relevant to issues of work performance and only pursuant to strict conditions of confidentiality in accordance with the Wigmore rules. Therefore, disclosure was permitted solely to the employer's counsel and medical experts, and only after the union and the grievor had a chance to black out irrelevant material.[12]

10.3 DISCLOSURE TO OTHER THIRD PARTIES

In balancing access to information against privacy rights, a British Columbia adjudicator has determined that where information from a public record cannot be disclosed but can be reasonably severed, an applicant is entitled to the remainder of the record. The onus is on the body to demonstrate that in the circumstances, it would not be reasonable to sever the record.[13] The mother of a boy who attended school in Nanaimo, British Columbia submitted two requests to the school board for disclosure of records pertaining to the boy's teacher in relation to investigations and hearings, results of a disciplinary hearing and a copy of any discussions from the hearing which the school board had sent to the College of Teachers.

The school board refused to confirm or deny whether the records had been sent to the College, as per section 8(2)(b) of the B.C. *Freedom of Information and Protection of Privacy Act* which permits public bodies to refuse to disclose records containing personal information about a third party if disclosure would be an unreasonable invasion of that party's privacy. The school board agreed to disclose hearing documents in severed form pertaining to personal information of the applicant and her son, but not the named teacher's employment history, in accordance with section 22(3)(d) of the Act, which prohibits disclosure of personal information relating to employment, occupational or educational history of a third party. The school also withheld documents that fell under section 12(3)(b) of the Act, which permits a public body to withhold the substance of deliberations of a meeting of its governing body where the meeting was held in private, and section 13(1), which allows a public body to refuse to disclose information that would reveal advice or recommendation developed by or for a public body

---

[12] Disability and Accommodation Reporter, September/October, 2004.
[13] Order 04-05, *Re Board of School Trustees of School District No. 68* (Nanaimo-Ladysmith); Office of the Information & Privacy Commissioner for British Columbia, February 16 2004.

or a minister. The applicant argued that the board had no right to sever the records and that the records should be disclosed pursuant to section 25(1) of the Act, which requires immediate disclosure of information where it relates to significant harm to the public and/or its disclosure is clearly in the public interest.

The adjudicator determined that the school board's refusal to confirm of deny whether it had submitted records to the College of Teachers was justified, as disclosure would unreasonably invade the teacher's privacy by revealing whether or not the school board had reported disciplinary action against the teacher under the B.C. *School Act*. The adjudicator also agreed with the board's decision to sever information containing the teacher's employment history, which included information regarding children other than the applicant's son, the teacher's own views and opinions, his work history and past performance, and the investigator's analysis and findings.

However, the adjudicator rejected the board's argument that it could withhold records in their entirety that were generated during *in camera* meetings, and requested that the board sever the brief references to the applicant and her son from the minutes of the meeting and disclose only that part of the document to the applicant. Further, the records that dealt specifically with the applicant and her son were held not to contain any explicit or implicit advice or recommendations to the school board, therefore, disclosure of these documents was permissible. With regard to the applicant's claim that immediate disclosure of information was required where it relates to significant public harm or is clearly in the public interest, the adjudicator held that there is no urgent or compelling need to disclose records without delay which concern an investigation into a teacher's workplace actions and behaviour.

In *Duncanson v. Toronto (Metropolitan) Police Services Board*,[14] the Ontario Divisional Court reviewed a decision by the Information and Privacy Commissioner of Ontario following her refusal of an appeal by two Toronto Star reporters from decisions made by the Metropolitan Toronto Police Services Board and the Ministry of the Attorney General. The reporters had requested from the Board disclosure of the names of all 5,000 police officers employed by the force, and information in relation to public complaints made against individual officers, including their names, ranks, the allegations made, the outcome of the complaints, and the docket sheets of the trials of all officers charged under the *Police Act*. From the Ministry, the reporters had requested disclosure of records of all *Criminal Code* charges laid against officers, including their names, their ranks, the charges and the disposition of the cases. The Commissioner had upheld the refusal

---

[14] (1999), [1999] O.J. No. 2464, 1999 CarswellOnt 2013 (Ont. Div. Ct.).

to disclose the records and the reporters brought an application for judicial review, seeking orders for disclosure of the records.

The Court dismissed the application for judicial review, upholding the Commissioner's refusal to disclose the names of all officers of the force on the basis that in certain circumstances, such disclosure could reasonably be expected to pose a threat to the health and safety of an officer and others, as per section 13 of the *Municipal Freedom of Information and Protection of Privacy Act*. The reporters had failed to show that the public interest in disclosure outweighed the need to protect police officers and others from serious threat to their health and safety. The Court also rejected the reporters argument that the police should have considered whether some of the officers' names could have been disclosed. It was not reasonable to expect the Board to sever the names of officers on the list who would not be endangered by the release of their names from those who would be, and it was within the discretion of the police to refuse the request in light of safety concerns. The Court held that although the Ministry did not provide reasons for refusing disclosure, the reporters were not prejudiced as this had not affected their ability to decide whether to appeal.

The issues in *Canada (Information Commissioner) v. Canada (Commissioner of the Royal Canadian Mounted Police)*[15] were similar and pertained to freedom of information and the right to inspect public documents containing personal information. In connection with litigation against four RCMP officers, an individual had requested information from the RCMP about the officers, including a list of the officers' historical postings, their status and date, the list of ranks and when they achieved those ranks, their years of service, their anniversary dates of service, and any public complaints made against the officers. The RCMP refused the request on the basis that the records constituted "personal information" as defined under section 3 of the *Privacy Act*, and therefore were exempt from disclosure pursuant to section 19(1) of the *Access to Information Act*.

The Federal Court of Appeal held that only information regarding a public servant's current or most recent position had to be released, however, on appeal to the Supreme Court of Canada, the Supreme Court ruled that although the information did qualify as "personal information" pursuant to the Act, the RCMP must disclose all of the information requested by the individual. The exception under section 3(j) of the *Privacy Act* applied, allowing disclosure because the information was directly related to the general characteristics associated with the position or function of a federal

---

[15] (Sub nom. *Canada (Information Commissioner) v. Canada (Commissioner of the Royal Canadian Mounted Police)*) [2003] 1 S.C.R. 66 (S.C.C.) [*Canada v. Commissioner of the RCMP*].

DISCLOSURE OF EMPLOYEE INFORMATION 10.3

employee. The information did not reveal anything about the competence of the officers or divulge any personal opinion given outside the course of employment, rather it provided information relevant to understanding the functions performed by the officers. The Court also held that the information applied retroactively and was not limited to an employee's most recent position.

At issue in *Dagg v. Canada (Minister of Finance)*[16] was whether the information in logs signed by employees entering and exiting the workplace on weekends constituted "personal information" as defined by section 3 of the Privacy Act, and whether the information should be disclosed pursuant to section 19(2)(c) of the *Access to Information Act* and section 8(2)(m)(i) of the *Privacy Act*. The logs were kept by security personnel only for safety and security reasons. Dagg filed a request with the Department of Finance for copies of the logs for the purpose of presenting the information to the union to assist them in the collective bargaining process, hoping that the union would be inclined to retain his services. While the logs were disclosed, the names, identification numbers and signatures of the employees were deleted. Dagg filed a complaint with the Information Commissioner, arguing that the deleted information should be disclosed in accordance with the section 3(j)(iii) exception of the *Privacy Act,* which provides for the disclosure of information about a federal employee relation to their position and functions including the classification, salary range, and responsibilities of the their position. The Federal Court, Trial Division ruled that the information did not constitute personal information, however, this decision was reversed by the Federal Court of Appeal.

On appeal to the Supreme Court of Canada, the Court interpreted the *Privacy Act* and *Access to Information Act* together to determine that the number of hours spent at the workplace was information relating to the position or function of federal employees, as it allowed for assessment of the amount of work required for a particular employee's position or function. As such, the information did relate to the "responsibilities of the position held by the employee" pursuant to section 3(j)(iii) of the *Privacy Act* and was accessible to the applicant under *the Access to Information Act*.

In *Dickie v. Nova Scotia (Department of Health)*[17] a patient in a provincial treatment facility requested access to information relating to an investigation of a facility employee and the decision taken pursuant to the investigation. The patient had alleged that the employee had engaged in an emotional and sexual relationship with her, thereby breaching his professional duties. Following the investigation, the Department of Health in-

---

[16] [1997] 2 S.C.R. 403 (S.C.C.).
[17] (1999), [1999] N.S.J. No.116, 1999 CarswellNS 97 (N.S. C.A.).

formed her that no disciplinary action could be taken against the employee. The patient then applied for access to information in relation to the investigation and was, per the decision of the Trial judge, granted access to much of the information, including names contained in the report, the employee's work-related conduct, and information communicated in confidence by other employees, as well as their names. The Department of Health appealed the Nova Scotia Supreme Court's decision.

The Nova Scotia Court of Appeal allowed the appeal in part, ruling that while the trial judge was correct in allowing the names to be disclosed, he erred in coming to this conclusion by limiting the definition of personal information instead of interpreting the language in a clear, broad and simple manner. The trial judge also erred in determining that the employee's work-related conduct did not relate to employment history, which constitutes personal information protected by the *Freedom of Information and Protection of Privacy Act*. The Court also held that the judge erred in finding that both the employee and other employees did not communicate their information in confidence. The disclosure of employees' and management's opinions and recommendations regarding the employee, and the employee's response to the allegations were presumed to be an unreasonable invasion of his personal privacy pursuant to the Act. The Court concluded that the types of information which should be disclosed to the complainant were the steps followed in the investigation, the names of employees who provided statements, communications by the patient to them regarding her allegations, and the decision made in relation to the employee over the allegations.

At issue in an application for review filed with the Nova Scotia Freedom of Information and Protection of Privacy Review Office was whether section 20 of the Nova Scotia *Freedom of Information and Protection of Privacy Act* supports the decision of the Department of Education to deny access to the agendas of the Minister and Deputy Minister of Education.[18] The applicant had requested a review of the Department's decision to deny access to all schedules, organizers, planners, agendas, and calendars of the Minister and Deputy Minister over a five-month period from May to September, 2001. The Department claimed an exemption to disclose such information pursuant to section 20(1) of the Act, which obliges a public body to refuse to disclose personal information if disclosure would be an unreasonable invasion of personal privacy, and suggested that it may be unsafe to allow the public to view how these individuals conduct their work throughout the day, including their location and patterns. Further, the Department argued that under section 20(3)(d), the information in the agendas

---

[18] Report FI-01-138, [2002] N.S.F.I.P.P.A.R. No. 4.

DISCLOSURE OF EMPLOYEE INFORMATION   10.3

related to employment history in a daily sense, and therefore qualified as personal information which should be exempted from disclosure.

Following previous decisions by both the British Columbia and Ontario Information and Privacy Commissioners, the Nova Scotia review officer noted the widely accepted distinction between personal information and professional information about public servants and individuals holding official positions in organizations. The review officer accepted that as a general rule, records containing information associated with an individual in the normal course of performing his or her professional or employment responsibilities is not personal information, nor is it personal information when his or her name appears on the record in relation to their functions as public employees.

With respect to the Department's claim for exemption of the agendas under employment history, the officer held that permitting the exemption would allow for too broad a definition of "employment history" and could potentially encompass job position, remuneration, or all employment-related interests, thereby conflicting with section 20(4)(e) which states that disclosure of such information is not an unreasonable invasion of privacy. Further, the officer stated that "employment history" refers only to past employment, rather than aspects of current employment such salary or job position.

While the review officer acknowledged that agendas could include reminders of doctor's appointments and social outings for which disclosure would constitute an unreasonable invasion of personal privacy or involve safety concerns and therefore should not be disclosed, he rejected the Department's assertion that agendas are by definition records of personal information. As such, each document must be considered individually and considered on its own merits regardless of its label, and a careful balancing act between the public's right to access information and the employee's right to privacy is required. The review officer concluded that objective facts recorded in public servants' agenda regarding their activities in the normal course of performing work responsibilities are not personal information about identifiable individuals and therefore must be disclosed to the applicant.

(For additional case law regarding disclosure of personal information of employees to third parties, see Chapter 3 — **Personnel Files**, Chapter 4 – **Work Product**, and Chapter 5 – **Personal Opinions**).

11

Conclusion

The many topics covered in this book have illustrated the breadth and complexity of privacy issues that arise or could arise in employment in the future. Case law highlights the challenges that Commissioners, arbitrators, and judges face when contemplating the employee's need to preserve basic privacy rights, in view of the employer's concern over ensuring the efficient and profitable functioning of their organization. While an employer has the right of direction and control of their employees in the workplace pursuant to the employment contract, the employee has an equal and inherent right to privacy and dignity in the course of employment. The adjudicator's job is to weigh these competing standpoints in a fair and impartial manner. The one certainty in every analysis is that no party's rights are absolute. Fundamental principles also prevail within the employer-employee relationship which must be considered in the context of workplace privacy, particularly in relation to surveillance, such as the employees' duty of loyalty to their employer, the employer's vicarious liability for an employee's activities, and the employer's obligation not to abuse their control and direction over employees.

Adding to the tension between the often countervailing interests of employees and employers is the notion that privacy has become one of the most important human rights of the modern age and is protected not only in our patchwork of Canadian privacy laws, but also around the world in diverse regions and cultures and in international agreements, namely, the Universal Declaration of Human Rights, the International Covenant on Civil and Political Rights, and the European Convention on Human Rights.[1] The Preamble to the Australian Privacy Charter upholds that "A free and democratic society requires respect for the autonomy of individuals, and limits on the power of both state and private organizations to intrude on that autonomy . . . Privacy is a key value which underpins human dignity and other key values such as freedom of association and freedom of speech. . . .

---

[1] Privacy International, "PHR2004 – Overview of Privacy", November 2004 at 56. online: <http://www.privacyinternational.org./article.shtml>.

CONCLUSION

Privacy is a basic human right and the reasonable expectation of every person."[2]

Nevertheless, advances in science and technology have facilitated the collection of employees' personal information and the monitoring of employee's performance and behaviour. Volumes of valuable personal information can be collected and scrutinized by employers through job interviews, references, background checks, psychological and intelligence tests, drug, medical and genetic tests, software programs, and workplace surveillance. In actual fact, employees themselves are assisting with this process, either as a condition of their employment, or in accordance with the employers' position that an employer is entitled to assert control over the workplace and their employees and ensure workplace productivity.[3]

Through our discussion of case law and privacy legislation, we have attempted to address some of the principal legal, social and policy issues that have emerged and will continue to emerge from the collection, use and disclosure of personal information in employment, issues that reveal significant implications in the workplace pertaining to matters of discrimination, exploitation, harassment, abuse of authority, breaches of confidentiality, and employee misconduct, to name a few. The struggle between employee and employer to control personal information takes place within the unique context of an ongoing and interdependent work relationship, wherein it is often in the best interests of both parties to preserve this association. Our review indicates that in the result, it is necessary to monitor both parties' behaviour as it relates to privacy in the workplace in order to equitably balance their respective interests and assist them to appropriately maintain their legal, social and economic relationship.

---

[2] *Ibid.*
[3] *Ibid.*